THE
ART OF
WINNING

THE
ART OF
WINNING

TEN LESSONS IN
LEADERSHIP, PURPOSE AND POTENTIAL

DAN CARTER

E

1

Ebury Edge, an imprint of Ebury Publishing
20 Vauxhall Bridge Road
London SW1V 2SA

Ebury Edge is part of the Penguin Random House group of companies
whose addresses can be found at global.penguinrandomhouse.com

Copyright © Dan Carter 2023

Dan Carter has asserted his right to be identified as the author of this
Work in accordance with the Copyright, Designs and Patents Act 1988

First published in the UK by Ebury Edge and in Australia and New Zealand
by Penguin Random House New Zealand in 2023

www.penguin.co.uk

A CIP catalogue record for this book is available from the British Library

Hardback ISBN 9781529146196
Trade Paperback ISBN 9781529146202

Printed and bound in Great Britain by Clays Ltd, Elcograf S.p.A.

The authorised representative in the EEA is Penguin Random House Ireland,
Morrison Chambers, 32 Nassau Street, Dublin D02 YH68

Penguin Random House is committed to a
sustainable future for our business, our readers
and our planet. This book is made from Forest
Stewardship Council® certified paper.

For Honor, Marco, Fox, Rocco and Cruz – navigating the way into this next chapter of my life hasn't been easy, and I know I couldn't have done it without you

CONTENTS

PART I

Repurposing

Knowing when it's time to make a change can be the hardest thing to get right in life. Walking towards something new inevitably means walking away from what you have now. Sometimes that's an easy decision: a better job, a bigger house. But walking away from something you value isn't so simple. It might mean leaving a career that provides much-needed security but lacks inspiration, uprooting your family from an area you like to move jobs, or exiting a project you believe in but which isn't playing out in the way you'd hoped.

What if it meant walking away from the role you'd spent your whole life working towards? Would you know when was the right time to call it a day and move on? Would it be the most difficult decision of your life? Or might you leave it too long, until the decision was taken out of your hands?

This is the moment that faces every professional sportsperson all too soon in their life. At a time when many people are contemplating the next step in their career, working hard towards achieving their goals, those of us in sport are contemplating the end. Will it be a career-ending injury? The dreaded tap on the shoulder from the coach? Or will we get to choose the manner of our departure? Everyone wants a fairy-tale ending: only a privileged few achieve it.

I was no different. I first thought seriously about retirement in 2013, at the age of thirty-one. Suffering from constant injuries, I felt that my body was giving up on me, no longer able to cope with the demands of professional rugby. But retirement was a dirty word to me, conjuring up the kind of images no one needs in their head: *Washed up. Has-been. No good anymore.* I dreaded retirement, feared it, avoided it at all costs.

So I found a way back. I became one of the privileged few. In 2015, the All Blacks team I'd been a part of for more than twelve years won the Rugby World Cup, and I had one of the best games I'd ever played in the black jersey. I got my fairy-tale ending.

You might think success at the highest level insulates you from the doubt. It would be easy to assume it makes it easier to decide when to call it a day, to draw a line under your own legacy. After all, with two World Cups and a glittering career with the All Blacks behind me, what did I have left to prove? But nothing could be further from the truth. My international career had ended, but I didn't want to finish playing. Like anyone who devotes themselves completely to a discipline and becomes hooked on the buzz that success brings, I couldn't imagine a life without rugby, and I had other things I wanted to achieve in the game.

Over the course of the next five years there were plenty of times when I thought I *should* retire – but that fear of retirement, that worry about what came next drove me to come back ever stronger. After all, what was the alternative? *Washed up. Has-been. No good anymore.*

In 2015 I went to play in France, for Racing 92, where we had some incredible success, winning the Top 14, France's domestic championship, in my first season and evolving the culture of the club. But the spectre of retirement was never far away: I suffered a serious injury in my third and final season with Racing 92, at the age of thirty-six. Was it time to go?

No amount of physical pain could match the depths of my dread about retirement. I *knew* I could do the rehab because I'd done it so many times before; I didn't have that same certainty about life after rugby. So I went through a brutal rehab regime and came back.

When I returned, I'd lost my place in the team and had to settle for a spot on the bench. But I learned to adapt to a new role within the squad rather than face up to the writing on the wall. And then I joined Kobe Steelers in Japan, on what I knew would be my final contract, where I was reunited with my coach and mentor Wayne Smith. We won the Japanese Top League in my first season, and I felt I was playing great rugby again.

By now I knew the inevitable was just around the corner, and it was all about finishing on my terms. So when the opportunity to return to France as an injury replacement came up, I jumped at the chance. *Any excuse to continue playing.* And when I failed the medical and learned I needed surgery on my neck, my immediate thought was, *It's time to give up.* It was a thought shared by the people closest to me. 'What have you got left to prove?' they asked.

Washed up. Has-been. No good anymore.

I found a way back again. Bowing out to an injury like this wasn't me controlling my destiny. And even as the doubts filled my head once again when I returned to Japan for my second season, leaving my family behind in New Zealand, I was determined to have an even better year than my first. To finish on a high.

Then the pandemic struck.

When the decision was eventually taken to cancel the Japanese Top League season I was distraught. In that moment, I lost all perspective. I didn't think about the bigger picture – the people going through much worse around the world, my privileged position to be insulated from the worst of it with my family in New Zealand. I'd lost my head and all I could think was that I wasn't going to be able to finish on my own terms. I was in a state of red – angry, confused, unable to take it in.

I stormed into my boys' bedroom, and my son Fox, five at the time, who is a sensitive soul and has a huge heart, knew immediately that something was up.

'What's wrong, Daddy?' he asked.

'They just cancelled the season on us,' I said.

'What does that mean?'

'It means I'm not going back to Japan.'

I was expecting him to say, 'Ah, that sucks, hard luck.' But instead a smile broke out across his face. 'That's the best news I've ever heard,' he said, and gave me a huge hug.

Suddenly, everything was put into perspective for me. Hearing this from my son, a five-year-old whose only take is that he gets to have his dad around again, crystallised the thoughts that had been swirling around my head for years now. *When is the right time to go?* I was an ageing athlete who had achieved everything I'd wanted to in the game. What exactly were my reasons for wanting to continue playing?

I thought back to myself at the same age, falling in love with the game during the inaugural Rugby World Cup. And I thought to my place now, to have spent so many years pursuing my goal to be the best player in the world. First to training, last to leave: if you want to be the best you have to do these things. But how do you reconcile that with trying to be the best parent you can be too? You have to be around, for starters.

I found the decision to retire so difficult, despite all my success, that it took an unprecedented set of global circumstances and the unvarnished truth from a five-year-old boy to make me see that I was finding any excuse to keep playing to avoid retirement. But there was nowhere to hide anymore, and over the course of that year I came to accept that my days as a professional rugby player were over.

I'm prone to introspection. Time without purpose is dangerous for me. I'd worked with some of the top mental skills coaches in the world, but always on the pursuit of greatness in the rugby environment. Never on the small matter of what I was planning on doing with the rest of my life after rugby. I hadn't had this much time to think since the injury lay-offs I'd experienced during my career, when it becomes a daily battle to put the dark thoughts to one side, to stop yourself becoming overwhelmed by the enormity of the road ahead and simply *focus on the process*. Do the next thing. Then the next thing. But at least with injuries there was always a destination, a goal I was working towards. With retirement there was nothing but the long road ahead, and I had no idea where it was leading.

I wasn't even thirty-eight yet. I still felt vital, that I had much to contribute to the world. But I was weighed down by that word, *retirement*. The whole foundation of my identity had been taken from me. *If I'm not Dan Carter, rugby player, then who am I?*

Throughout my playing career I'd always known what my purpose was. When I got out of bed each day I was striving to improve upon the player I was yesterday, to be the best rugby player in the world. My purpose involved being first to training, last to leave. It meant setting relentless standards for myself. And it also demanded great sacrifice: at times putting my career and my pursuit of excellence first, and my family second.

That feels like quite a shocking thing to write, especially as a dedicated family man and father to four, but it's a truth that anyone who has walked the road in pursuit of high performance will know. Alongside this purpose, I had everything structured: training, meetings, nutrition, exercise, travel, doctors and health and wellbeing staff from across the spectrum, all laid on for me. I had teammates and camaraderie, coaches who challenged me and supported me. My years were a packed calendar of matches and tournaments. Even my time off was scheduled, monitored, structured.

And then it all just stops.

I know I'm in a fortunate position to have had a long and successful career, to be in good health and not face the financial and physical troubles many players face upon retirement. But it is still a huge social adjustment to make to my perceived 'normal' life – similar to what I imagine those in the armed forces make when they retire from service. And, if I'm honest, I have to say I struggled with it.

I felt rudderless without a purpose driving me. There was a huge void inside me that rugby had filled, and I looked forward and wondered, *What is going to replace that over the next ten, twenty, thirty years?* Having achieved so much on the rugby field, how could I hope to come close to matching that in the next stage in my career?

And then there was the anxiety, the self-doubt. I'd dabbled in business during my sports career, but if that was where I saw a future, where would I fit in? I never went to university, and a part of me had always thought, *I don't deserve to be in these important business meetings. I'm not smart enough. My input doesn't matter because I'm just a rugby player.* I questioned whether I was good enough – whether I even deserved to be in a boardroom – because I wasn't educated to what I imagined to be a high enough standard.

I knew I had to get some help to deal with this transition in my life – I couldn't do it on my own. I was in the privileged position of being able to call upon a lot of great people to talk to – including many former teammates who had gone through the same transition, and some former sports people who had gone on to have great success in their second careers. Perhaps the most important connection I made during this time was with Kevin Roberts, a former CEO of Saatchi & Saatchi who does a lot of consultancy work with top sports teams and players, including the All Blacks in the past.

Kevin had a process that could be of great value to me, he told me: 'It will be confrontational, hard work and challenging. Are you going to commit to this?'

'You're damn right,' I replied. 'I'm all in.'

And so began a process that is still ongoing in my life, a process that has forced me to look inwardly in a way I've never had to before, that has proven challenging, frustrating, rewarding and left me full of gratitude. It's a process that I've given name to for this part of my life:

*I'm not in retirement. I'm in the process of **repurposing**.*

Through this process of repurposing, firstly through Kevin's help and then with that of others and on my own, I have tried to establish my own set of beliefs and values, looking back through my life so far and finding what really resonated with me. In particular, I looked back at my career in rugby and asked myself, *What exactly is it that you love about this game and want to take into the next chapter of your life?*

There was the strong work ethic, of course – players love getting their hands dirty. The teamwork, team ethos – I wouldn't want to be a player in an individual sport – the idea of no individual being bigger than the team. I loved the value of always wanting to give back to the game: grassroots rugby, community rugby, youth rugby. The idea of never forgetting where you came from. It's why I love going back to my home town of Southbridge.

Then there was the spirit of rugby: to go to war for eighty minutes and build friendships after – some of my best friends now are opponents from my playing days. I don't think that happens in all sports. That's because of the respect. No egos, just respect for your teammates, opponents, fans and refs. And I loved the social diversity: the fact that everyone can play the game – different shapes, sizes, religions; boys and girls, old and young. It's a very inclusive sport, I feel.

But what really came to me was remembering myself as a five-year-old boy, watching the inaugural Rugby World Cup on TV in 1987. I remember going straight out into the garden and copying the feats of players like John Kirwan, Michael Jones and David Kirk, images of them on the TV stamped on my memory even now. And then later, as a young player looking up to players like Andrew Mehrtens, Christian Cullen and Jonah Lomu. I look back at the impact those icons had on me as a kid, and now, when reviewing my own career, it isn't the three World Rugby Player of the Year awards or two World Cups I'm most proud of, it's the impact I've had on the next generation. The idea that somehow I might have inspired a young person the way these players did for me is incredible.

So, through the process of taking a journey through my career and all the ups and downs I'd seen through eighteen years in the game, the idea for this book was born.

I began to realise that my anxieties about my education existed only in my mind. I had an education of another kind to draw upon, as part of the unbelievable culture of excellence in the All Blacks. I'd experienced the thrill of winning the World Cup and playing a Test match back in 2005 against the Lions that people still talk about to this day, but I'd also tasted the kind of defeat that never quite leaves you, suffered with injuries and made regrettable mistakes off the field. I'd executed skills and held my nerve in high-pressure situations in front of thousands of spectators in stadiums, with millions more watching at home on TV. I'd developed from being a naïve, quiet kid at the start of my career to taking on one of the key leadership positions in the team. I'd grown and evolved. I'd fought back from setbacks, becoming incredibly resilient in the process. My experiences held value not only in rugby, but beyond.

My confidence grew when organisations like AstraZeneca, who were trying to develop a Covid vaccine at the time, and a team at the Nuffield Department of Surgical Sciences, part of the University of Oxford, wanted to hear my thoughts on managing pressure. I also spoke in Paris with the general managers of Louis Vuitton, at the invitation of their CEO, Michael Burke, about the importance of humility in a team environment. And then when organisations like the Oxford Foundry asked me to get involved in helping to mentor their next generation of leaders, when people showed interest in learning about the kind of resilience I'd built up through coming back from setbacks in my career, I felt certain that I had something to offer after all.

That 'something' forms the content of this book, ten high-performance lessons – and, having played as number 10 for most of my career, it had to be ten – I'd like to share from my time in rugby. These aren't my Ten Commandments inscribed in stone, but rather ten chapters of insight and experience I'm offering in the hope that, no matter what walk of life you're in, you can take something from. Whether you're a business looking to work on your culture, a leader on a steep learning curve, a person navigating change in their life or just someone of any age trying to get that little bit better every day, I hope that my experience can spur you on to greater heights, just as the people I grew up admiring inspired me.

Through the ten chapters we will look at:

1. The power of **personal and collective purpose**, and how the All Blacks environment produced the perfect synergy of the two to deliver back-to-back World Cups.
2. Using the **knowledge of your past** to create meaning in your culture and success: in where you've come from lies the key to where you're going.
3. Why **pressure is a privilege** and walking towards it is the only way to tame it.
4. **Focusing on the process** to help stay in the here and now.
5. How going from good to great is tough, but **great to great** is even harder.
6. Why **mind control** is the key to winning on and off the field.
7. How setbacks help build the **resilience** of winning cultures.
8. **Empowering your people** to make their own decisions and drive their own culture.

9. The importance of humility and bringing your **real self, not ideal self** to play, whether on or off the pitch.

10. **Gratitude**, and why it pays for us all to smile and say thanks once in a while.

One idea that I kept returning to during this time was the idea of winning being an art. It isn't a science – there's no exact formula you can concoct to guarantee success. And yet you don't just stumble across it. You have to learn as you go, try new things and evolve – I was a very different player at the end of my career than I was at the beginning, finding new ways to win and to lead. For me it was more an art than a strategy, and with this book, *The Art of Winning*, I'd like to open the doors on the culture of excellence that is the All Blacks and share with you the tools and lessons I took through my eighteen years of playing professional rugby. I'm at the starting line of the next stage of my career, not the finishing line, and I'm excited about what the future holds. It's a challenge I'm thrilled to walk towards – so come and join me as you navigate both your present and your future, and use the Art of Winning to inspire your next step.

PART II

The Ten Lessons

Everyone wants to win. But that isn't a purpose, it's a goal. Your purpose is something beyond that.

CHAPTER 1

PURPOSE

When I look back on my career, I keep returning to an image I have of myself as a five-year-old boy, out in the backyard kicking goals. That boy fell in love with rugby properly for the first time during the 1987 Rugby World Cup in Australia and New Zealand, sitting with his dad and watching heroes like John Kirwan scoring a try, Grant Fox directing the play with his kicking and David Kirk holding aloft the Webb Ellis Cup. That five-year-old was straight out in the back garden, replicating Kirwan's magic with the ball in hand, kicking vital goals and sowing the seeds of a dream that would endure throughout his childhood – to be an All Black.

In 2003 that dream became a reality. I never actually thought it would, growing up in a country town of only 750 people. But at the age of twenty-one, I played my first game for the All Blacks, against Wales in Hamilton, and I came off the pitch at the end of the game having scored twenty points, a dream debut. It would have been easy at that point to simply walk off the pitch, give myself a pat on the back and think, *OK, cool, what's next?* But, instead, I was filled with the feeling that this wasn't enough. It wasn't enough simply to achieve my dream.

This experience of being an All Black was so special, so unique that I didn't want it to stop. I knew as I walked from the pitch, shaking hands with the opposition, congratulating my teammates and soaking up the atmosphere, that it was never going to be enough for me to play a few matches or just a season or two as an All Black. I knew I wanted more. I'd never been more sure of anything.

I didn't just want to be an All Black. *I wanted to strive to be an All Black great.*

THE POWER OF PERSONAL PURPOSE

It's only now that I look back at my childhood and understand that the boy I was then was, without even knowing it, playing with purpose. All of the hours spent 'practising', if such a word is even accurate for doing something you love – kicking in the garden until only the fading light or bedtime stopped me, playing age-grade rugby, spending weekends at Southbridge Rugby Club – were all because I loved rugby. But that dream to be an All Black was always there, without me really thinking too much about it, and that purpose subconsciously guided me. As a child, it comes naturally to have a beginner's mindset, to embrace new challenges and constantly seek growth. I've had a lot of great coaches in my time, but during the hours I spent kicking, making adjustments, trying new techniques, making my own kicking tees, it was all pure pleasure, but I was also coaching myself. Improving as a kicker each and every day.

For me, a growth mindset is simply the idea that we believe we are capable of being better than we were yesterday, and that we strive to make that improvement each and every day, so that it becomes habit. It often seems to come naturally to us as children, but as we get older, we need a growth mindset just as much if we're to constantly evolve and improve. If we're at all serious about achieving our potential then it's absolutely vital. But without our childhood innocence, that natural learning curve we're all on as children, it can be more challenging. We have to approach it in a more conscious, concerted way. So, when I walked off the pitch with that thought, *I want to be an All Black great*, I needed to also ask myself: *OK, so what does an All Black great do?*

Through exploring the answer, I was able to create a set of values that would remain consistent throughout my career, even as circumstances and my style of play changed. I decided that an All Black great:

1. Has to play consistently over several years – potentially more than a decade – not just a couple of Tests or seasons.
2. Needs to constantly evolve his game and improve to develop as a player and beat off all challengers.
3. Adheres to world-class standards and works harder than his teammates and opponents.
4. Makes sacrifices in his life to make sure his purpose comes first.

The discovery of this sense of personal purpose was an incredibly liberating and focusing moment for me. It would provide a constant torch for me to follow, a guiding light through which to filter any major decision, setback or distraction in my life. I would come to think of it like swimming in a lane of a pool. Either side of you are the lane markers and along the bottom is the centre line, which would function as my purpose. You might be swimming your heart out but find yourself veering off course without realising, so the lane markers either side of you would remind you that you were heading towards the other lane, and the centre line would bring you back to where you needed to be.

But more than this, my purpose provided a higher calling, something beyond simply winning the next game, playing the best I could in the next Test – it allowed me to strive for greatness. And, as I would discover later, this purpose is what kept me going when life intervened and moved the goalposts in my career – which happens to all of us at some time or another – and my ambitions seemed impossibly far away.

One thing it didn't allow me to do was cruise. I might wake up one morning, feeling a little sore and tired from the day before, thinking maybe I'd skip my recovery that day. But through asking, *What would an All Black great do?* I would quickly see that wasn't an option.

Of course, it's one thing to discover a purpose, but it's quite another to strive towards it every single day. To do that requires dedication, consistency and vast reserves of self-belief. But first and foremost, it requires patient and meticulous planning.

_____

FAIL TO PREPARE, PREPARE TO . . .

With my long-term purpose in place, and the values I needed to aspire to in order to achieve that purpose – the *why*, if you like – I then had to look at the *how*: exactly what I needed to do. I had to break that ten-year-ish aim down into smaller parts, with their own individual goals, starting with the year ahead.

I would set goals I wanted to achieve for the year and look at the campaigns I needed to be a part of to achieve those goals. So, in a typical year, I might sit down in January and look ahead: I knew that to achieve my goals I needed to be on the end-of-year tour, part of the Tri Nations, the June or July series for the All Blacks, but first and foremost to have a good Super Rugby season with the Crusaders. I would look at it with a really broad overview, and I would then look at the campaign directly in front of me: *Right, it's January. Super Rugby: forget all those other competitions.*

What are my goals for Super Rugby? I'd ask myself, and then I'd work my socks off to achieve them, which would then give me the best chance of being in the next campaign. The key to this, however, was to be upfront and completely transparent with my coaches about the Super Rugby season, so that I became accountable for my goals.

I'd always start with the individual campaigns: if it was a World Cup year, for example, or that season's southern hemisphere Tri Nations or autumn Test series. I'd set goals for each campaign, so that everything I did leading up to and during the competitions would be focused on achieving these, and then I'd look at goals for the individual matches.

So, for one game the goal might be to 'be an attacking first five-eighth'. How do I go about that? I'd need to play flat on the line, do extra speed work, analyse the opposition through this prism.

Through having these goals I'd be able to plan what I needed to do every week, then every day within that. Every Sunday evening, I would sit down with my notebook and plan out the week ahead, all with my goals and purpose in mind. Training was regimented of course, but I would map out the extra work I did beyond that: my extra kicking sessions three or four times a week, which varied but sometimes meant a hundred kicks a week; my pool recovery and massage the day after a game; meetings with the physio, the nutritionist. I would even plan my days off. I didn't want to waste a single day of my week, and I'd put in family time for the morning, perhaps a thirty-minute swim in the afternoon: planning each day so that I could say from that first long-term purpose I was breaking things down by year, month, week and day to give manageable, achievable tasks that allowed me to concentrate on what I was doing in the moment and yet build eventually towards that long-term vision.

Purpose → Goals for the year ahead → The competition ahead → The game ahead → The day ahead

One thing to be clear about, though, is that I never wanted to plan too far ahead. There's no point sitting down in January to map out your goals for a Tri Nations series in August, when you still have the Super Rugby season to come first. If you're not fully focused on the next thing in front of you then it can have an impact on your performance, it can mean you take things for granted, you take your eye off the ball – and you just can't afford to do that if you're on the path to high performance. Play poorly in Super Rugby and there'll be no Tri Nations. And that's before you factor in things like injuries, which can derail the best-laid plans of anyone and force long-term aims to be adapted.

So, I would break down my preparation for Super Rugby, and if I achieved my goals and the team achieved its goals, I would then be in a position to get selected for the All Blacks. It's like step one of a five-step process for the year. Super Rugby, my first step, is done, and now it's time for step two, the June/July Test series for the All Blacks. And I'd go through the process again: ask myself, what do I want to achieve in this competition? Then I'd share that aim with my coaches, hold myself accountable to it, and then plan it out. And on it goes, planning each step but with the knowledge that none of it means anything if you don't deliver on the next thing in front of you.

This level of preparation appeals to my nature: I love planning and being super-organised, and it was a quality that was fully encouraged in the All Blacks environment. When head coach Graham Henry and his team, including his assistant coaches Wayne Smith and Steve Hansen, took over in 2004, they pushed for us to get planning and be prepared. 'Why do you think you can come to a meeting and remember everything?'

Wayne Smith would say. 'You need your book to write things down and do your homework.'

This might all sound a little prescriptive, a bit like school, and some players would certainly use their books and write and plan more than others. But I believe the discipline required to do this is what allowed me to be the player I was. If I did all the work in the week, from the planning to the training and everything in between, then it allowed me to go out and play at the weekend with freedom. Yes, there'd be nerves, but I knew I'd done the work, which gave me confidence, and now it was time to go out there and just play – I had the confidence to express myself and trust my instincts.

Of course, this level of planning is itself open to the temptation to cruise sometimes. At eight o'clock on a Sunday evening it's often easy to think, *Do I really want to spend my evening planning the week ahead? Maybe I could sack it off, spend some time with the boys . . .*

And that's when revisiting my personal purpose would come in: *What would an All Black great do?* An All Black great would do his preparation. And by doing it consistently it becomes a habit rather than an unwanted distraction.

Of course, within a professional sports environment, it is easier to plan everything to the minute because it's so much more regimented than life in other disciplines. But this structure, from purpose to goals to *how*, is, I believe, one of the keys to high performance and is something that can be carried over into anyone's life, no matter what their occupation or goals. In my life now, after rugby, I still map out my week ahead and maintain this meticulous approach to planning.

And at the end of each week I review the week that was before planning the next week. Sometimes I will have reached my goals the preceding week, but sometimes I won't, and part of this review is to ask why. There might be circumstances outside of your control that are to blame – as a player things like injury or losing a game despite putting in a good performance – but it might also be because I simply have not done the things that I said I was going to do. And that's not high performance. That's cruising.

But as my wife, Honor, will attest, there's a fine line between being well organised and a control freak, and it's vital to adapt to the context, to be clear about when it's necessary. When Covid first hit and I returned home from Japan, the schools soon closed as the whole country went into lockdown. With the kids at home I thought, *Right, if we're home-schooling, I'm going to do it to a world-class standard.* I brought the full weight to bear of my eighteen years as a professional rugby player, micro-managing the week ahead with breakfast at eight o'clock, maths at nine, snack breaks, free time – scheduling it all just like a training week with the All Blacks had been for me.

Of course, it was a disaster. On the first day the kids were screaming, 'We don't want to do this!' And I'd taken on the role of Sergeant Major: 'Come on, guys – this has to be world class!' My mindset was that I had to deliver the best home-schooling system in the world, but by the end of the day Honor said, 'What are you doing? They're kids. This is home – it isn't school. Kids need to be kids.'

But while the Dan Carter method of home-schooling has been put to bed for ever, the tools I used during my time playing rugby haven't. Being a professional rugby player means having your time planned and managed for optimal performance: gym sessions, meetings, travel, even twenty-minute sleeps are built into your daily plan. I loved that and thrived on the detail, but now, outside of rugby, I still make a lot of notes and plan, just with a bit more freedom. I still spend Sunday planning the week ahead, looking at what I want to achieve, but now it's more with a to-do list for every day, setting goals I want to achieve for the week and scheduling my training plan. Just like when I played rugby, I like to go into the weekend knowing I've done the work – I've earned my beer. If I've only done 50 per cent of what I set out to do, I don't feel that that's achieving. It's not high performance – it's accepting mediocrity, which isn't in my make-up, and if you're serious about improving, doesn't have a place in yours.

DO YOU HAVE A PERSONAL PURPOSE IN YOUR LIFE?

Do you have something that brings you back to the centre of your lane when you're at risk of veering off? Can you express it in a sentence? Finding your purpose can be the easy part – or the hard part, depending on how naturally it comes to you. But once you have established your personal purpose, you need to set about looking at *how* you can strive towards it.

In 2021 I was appointed the first Leader in Practice by the Oxford Foundry, the entrepreneurship centre at the University of Oxford. It was a fantastic opportunity for me to share my knowledge and experiences from rugby and help inspire the next generation of entrepreneurs and leaders. And it gave me the chance to talk with Reid Hoffman, founder of the Oxford Foundry and one of the most successful entrepreneurs in the world. As part of our discussion, Reid told me about the importance of 'poetry and plumbing' in leadership, which he explained as 'the poetry is the great idea and the plumbing is how we actually get it done'.

It struck me as an expression that could equally be applied to your purpose. The purpose, of course, would be the poetry: 'to be an All Black great', in my case, 'to be world-class at my job' or 'to be a compassionate and effective leader' or 'to get a little better every day than I was yesterday' could be others more appropriate for you. It might even be 'to change the world'! For businesses and organisations, the philosophy is the same. For Adidas, their poetry is: 'Through sport, we have the power to change lives'. For UNICEF, it's 'to save children's lives, to defend their rights, and to help them fulfil their potential, from early childhood through adolescence. And we never give up.' And while Reid Hoffman didn't spell out his personal purpose to me in so many words, he did talk about the mission of a start-up needing founders to ask themselves, 'Why is the world you're trying to change to better than this one?' This is the kind of big question that comes from big ambitions.

Once you have your poetry, you then have to look at the plumbing: *How do I get that done?*

For me, of course, the plumbing took the form of my planning ahead, focusing most keenly on the next task in front of me, and the discipline and hard work required to constantly follow this purpose. For you, it could be a case of looking ahead at the next six months to a year and breaking it down into your own 'campaigns' and setting goals for the months ahead. What are the key moments throughout your year that you need to target? What do you want to get out of these moments? If you work in a sales environment, it might mean targeting key periods of time when you can really shine – the run-up to Christmas, for example – or it could be geared towards things like an annual review, conferences throughout the year or opportunities for courses and education outside of your day job to strive towards your personal purpose.

So, you would look at these moments and then go about setting goals for them, tangible things you can hold yourself accountable for – or better yet, share with your manager or a colleague so that they can hold you accountable. Ask yourself *What do I want to get out of this moment?*

Always concentrate primarily on the goal in front of you and resist the temptation to divert too much focus too far ahead. Far too many sports teams to mention trip themselves up by looking too far ahead and getting complacent about **what's next**, and it's just as easy to do it in your own life. Break down your weeks and develop your own review process when you can explore what went well and what you can do to improve. I conduct mine every Sunday night, but you can find a time and frequency that works for you – and stick to it.

THE TEAM'S PURPOSE

When the All Blacks finally won the World Cup in 2011 at Eden Park, some twenty-four years since we'd last won the tournament at the same venue, it was a moment of great triumph and joy – and, it has to be said, relief. In many ways, it would have been easy to look at that moment as a finishing line of sorts, to have finally achieved something that had been beyond generations of teams before us. It's certainly human nature to relax after a moment like that, something borne out by the fact that, historically, there are many examples of teams winning the Rugby World Cup and failing to maintain those standards the following year.

We didn't want to be a statistic like that. We wanted to buck that trend, which demanded new goals and a new long-term vision, but we knew it wasn't going to be easy. After twenty-four years of not winning a World Cup, we were desperate for it, but it wasn't going to be as simple as saying, 'Let's go and win the next one in 2015' and settling on that as our goal, because subconsciously you can think, *Well, we won the last one, it probably doesn't matter as much if we don't win this one.* And this goal isn't going to provide enough intrinsic motivation on all the staging posts before the next

World Cup, the Tri Nations and tours. It isn't paving the road beyond the next World Cup.

What we needed was something longer than a four-year period to the next World Cup. Something that would likely still be in motion by the time some of us – me included – retired or moved on. We needed something that would recreate the feeling we had of being desperate to win a World Cup after twenty-four years.

When we're eight points down with five minutes to go, what's going to stop us from drifting towards that subconscious thought: *Well, we won the World Cup last year, it doesn't really matter if we don't win this?*

The answer lay in addressing our collective purpose. What's the team's purpose? Back-to-back World Cups is just a part of it. Staying number one in the world? Well, that's just a part of it too.

We had made the progression from being a good team to becoming a great one by winning the World Cup at last, a transition that business consultant and author Jim Collins describes for companies in his book *Good to Great*. But while going from good to great was one thing, what we were talking about was going from great to *great* – to follow success with success. Because that's the pinnacle of true greatness in any discipline: if you look at football and the Manchester United teams of Sir Alex Ferguson and more recently their City neighbours led by Pep Guardiola, these are teams that delivered back-to-back Premier League titles; tennis greats Serena Williams, Roger Federer, Rafa Nadal and Novak Djokovic each delivered back-to-back Grand Slam titles on numerous occasions; and Jamaican athletes Elaine Thompson-Herah and Usain Bolt each delivered back-to-back sprint doubles (the 100 and 200 metres gold medals) at consecutive Olympic Games. They went from great to great.

I still remember in the early months of 2012 being at the hotel in Christchurch with the All Blacks leadership group and the management, trying to work out how to go from great to great and avoid the blip that other teams go through, when our coach Steve Hansen came up with the purpose that would come to define the remainder of my time with the All Blacks:

'What about being the most dominant team in the history of world rugby?'

Woah. As humble Kiwis, that's not exactly the sort of thing we'd feel comfortable going around shouting about. But this simply expressed purpose struck a chord with all of us. We all bought into it (even if it was something we certainly wouldn't be going around telling anyone outside the team environment) – not just the players but the management and staff too. And, just as with my personal purpose, we started to look at what exactly *being the most dominant team in the history of world rugby* would look like. The plumbing for the poetry, if you like.

The first thing to be clear about here is that you're never going to achieve it. There's no mountain summit where you plant your flag and declare, *We've done it!* The purpose doesn't have an end point as such, but if you even find yourself in the conversation about what the most dominant team in history is, then you know you've gone some way to achieving it.

But back there in Christchurch, we looked at things like:

- It's a ten-year process.
- Being number one in the world for longer than anyone has been there before.
- Winning back-to-back World Cups – something no team in history had done before.
- Winning our first World Cup outside of New Zealand.
- Continuing to retain the Bledisloe Cup each year.

Suddenly we had these clear metrics to guide our way, thanks to a shared, collective purpose. As a player, you'd walk into the team room with that purpose clear in your mind. It would inform our decisions and be a clear and present influence on all of our actions. We were in this together, and while we might not all be around till its conclusion – whatever that might involve – we would all be pushing in the same direction, unified by our common purpose.

The purpose allowed for a huge shift in our vision but, vitally – and this is important in any organisation – it fitted with the key values of the All Blacks, which involved paying tribute to the history of the All Blacks and to *leave the jersey in a better place than when you received it*. Without these key values and new purpose aligning, the purpose simply won't stick. And, of course, without buy-in from those involved it isn't going to work either – which is why the marriage of personal and collective purpose is so important.

PERSONAL AND COLLECTIVE PURPOSE: A PERFECT PARTNERSHIP

When you're walking towards a purpose like ours, it's a process that takes several years. The temptation is to look too far ahead, to think, *Well, I won't be around in ten years*, and possibly switch off. That's why breaking it down and having complete buy-in from everyone concerned is so important.

With everyone from the coach to the physio buying into our collective purpose, it meant we were able to aspire to world-leading standards on a daily basis. It meant that the physio, for example, was able to look at themselves and ask: *If I'm going to be the physio for the most dominant team in the history of world rugby, what do I need to do each day to help the team strive for this?*

If people weren't living to these standards, they shouldn't be there. That might sound harsh, but you can't have passengers on the road to excellence. Because of the collected buy-in to the purpose, anyone failing to meet these standards was challenged. The team purpose had to come first, and this becomes so much easier when it marries with your personal purpose.

My purpose, to be an All Black great, was a perfect match for our collective purpose. It empowered me to be able to align my personal goals with the collective goals of the team, so that in a very real sense what was good for my own purpose was the same as what was good for the team. An All Black great wins back-to-back World Cups, but let's be clear, no All Black great in history has won a World Cup without an exceptional team around him.

One of the key All Black tenets is that **no individual is bigger than the team** – something we'll explore in greater depth later in the book – and at the heart of this is the idea that the team's purpose comes first. If a person's personal purpose is at odds with the collective purpose, if they think that their personal purpose comes first, they're going to make decisions that put themselves first and the team second. They're going to be selfish, possibly at key moments, and risk the integrity of the team's collective goals.

Of course, every player and every team want to win the World Cup or achieve whatever success in their respective field is relevant. Everyone wants to win. But that isn't a purpose, it's a goal. Your purpose is something beyond that. Wanting to get your bonus, successfully ask for a pay rise or get promoted are all goals you might have in your job, and they might be metrics you need to deliver on the road towards your purpose, but your purpose should be a loftier target. It should be long-term, something that will get you out of bed each day, something which will benefit not only you, but the organisation you're a part of.

So, your personal purpose might not immediately seem to be a perfect fit with the collective purpose, or perhaps the team's new purpose is a change in direction that initially causes you to call into question your role within it. If that's the case, then you need to look at how your personal purpose fits. Perhaps it requires you to evolve slightly and adapt so that you can fit in to the environment. But what's important is that you're able to find a way to align the two, with the knowledge that the team's purpose must come first. And if you're unable to find a way to align them, that's going to cause problems.

PIVOT: WHEN YOUR PURPOSE MUST EVOLVE

In 2015 I played my last ever game for the All Blacks, a World Cup final by the end of which we had made good on our ambition to become the first side to win back-to-back World Cups. But, of course, that wasn't the end point for the team or its purpose to be the most dominant team in the history of world rugby. It was simply the end of my involvement in helping the team strive towards that purpose. I'd been the custodian of the jersey and now it was someone else's turn to live up to those standards every day.

Of course, it also meant an end of sorts for the personal purpose I'd held for thirteen years, a purpose that had seen me evolve into a markedly different player to the one I'd been at the beginning, that had helped me through some pretty devastating lows and enabled me to reach some dizzying heights too. You never really stop being an All Black – a certain responsibility remains even after you've passed on the jersey – but now that I was no longer playing, it certainly made striving to be an All Black great a lot more challenging. Whether or not I'd actually achieved my purpose was up to others to decide, but I'd begun to see that *striving* towards that purpose was what mattered.

When I finished with the All Blacks, then, I needed to ask myself, *What is your personal purpose now?* It's a question I would be forced to return to in 2020 when I finished playing, without finding an answer quite so easily, but for now I knew I had ambitions to play in Europe, and I had a number of offers from teams, some of which had enjoyed success recently. Teams like Toulon had achieved incredible success with Jonny Wilkinson, Matt Giteau and Bryan Habana, to name a few. But I wanted to go somewhere that was aspiring to build a culture and was, like me, aiming to have a place at the top table of European rugby. I think I might have struggled for motivation at a team expected to continue success or one for which such success was unlikely.

So, my personal purpose became *to prove to myself and my teammates that I could achieve success in European rugby*, which married perfectly with the club I eventually signed for, Racing 92, which were regularly featuring in the top six of the championship but had huge aspirations to make the next step and be one of the top teams in Europe.

When you've achieved a lot of your goals in life, finding new ways to motivate yourself is the key to longevity, and a renewed purpose and set of goals is at the heart of it. When I went to a new team, I had a new sense of energy and purpose: I had to earn the respect of my new teammates, coaches and fans. I couldn't allow myself to think, *I've won a couple of World Cups, I can just relax, have a bad game, miss training . . .* I never had that mentality – I always felt I had to prove myself.

Later, in 2018 when I signed for Kobe Steelers in Japan, my

purpose adjusted in response to new concerns: I knew I was coming towards the end of my career and it was all about gratitude for me by this stage. Yes, the ambitions of the team were to win back-to-back titles and our purpose was to put in place the beginnings of a dynasty, all of which came first and we needed to be aligned with, but on a more personal level I was determined to enjoy these last years as a rugby player. I was determined to train as *smart* as I possibly could. If ever there was a day I didn't feel much like training, I would remind myself: *This is going to be one of your last ever training days. These are the final years you'll be able to call yourself a rugby player.*

It gave me a huge sense of motivation and direction, and my purpose became: *to finish on my terms – to finish on a high.* I had a piece of paper on my bedroom wall with the whole season on, and I would tick each game off as it came and went (ten to go . . . nine to go . . .) until my last game of rugby ever. It gave me such drive to know I was on the final stretch of this journey, and I wanted to make the most of every moment. Again, circumstances meant I didn't get to finish my second Japanese season, but what mattered wasn't the destination – it was that this was driving me.

Every time my purpose changed, it wasn't a case of complete overhaul, of ripping it up and starting again: it was a process of evolution, each renewed purpose adjusting to the realities of the stage of my career I was at, but with my core values and beliefs driving it and with consistent qualities always a part of it: *To be the best player I possibly could be. To get out of bed and believe that each day I could improve a little on the player I was yesterday. To help drive this team in any capacity I can.*

And that's why changing an effective purpose is always likely to be a gradual shift in course, because it involves remaining true to your values and beliefs, rather than a huge about turn that might run contrary to them. It's a process of evolution rather than revolution, and even when I hung up my boots and tried to discover my new purpose as part of a major change in direction, going from rugby player to where I am now, my core purpose was never going to be such a dramatic change in tone because it would always be something true to me.

FINDING YOUR PURPOSE CAN BE HARD

Walking off the rugby field at the end of my first game as an All Black and realising what my purpose was probably makes it sound like it was easy for me to discover it, and I wouldn't disagree with that. Sport is unlike the real world in many ways because it's built around clear metrics: win or lose. A successful kick or a missed effort. Striving to be an All Black great seemed the next logical step to me.

It's only really in retirement that I've truly come to appreciate just what a struggle discovering one's purpose can be. It's a process that has been confrontational and extremely challenging at times. When I started working with Kevin Roberts, we thought it would be a one-month to six-week process; it took six months.

As difficult and challenging as asking yourself, *Who am I?* and creating a purpose can be, I know from experience that the rewards can be huge. After working with Kevin, I found a niche at two of the companies I was involved in helping with their culture – Glorious Digital, an NFT marketplace; and Asuwere, a clothing subscription business. We went through the process of examining what our collective purpose was, but I went one step further and asked the key shareholders and leaders to address their own purpose, to ask themselves questions like: *Why are you part of the business? What are you going to bring to it?*

I really got them to break it down and then, crucially, made them accountable for it. I asked everyone to present theirs to the rest of the team. Some of them – people who have achieved great success in business – had never done it before. A couple of guys who had helped set up the businesses were in tears because they were that proud; it was the first time they had been asked to reflect on the team they had put together to help grow their businesses. It was a process that really broke down barriers and allowed people to get to know their teammates in new ways and understand their place within the culture. Crucially, through being vulnerable and honest with one another it felt like a great place to start things off: there was no bullshitting, and everyone knew they would be held to the standards of the purpose they shared going forward.

Just as in the All Blacks teams I played in, we had a collective purpose and then within that our own personal purpose, aligned with that of the collective. And making myself accountable for my purpose and goals was an essential part of that: I would share them with the coaches and work on them in the knowledge that by furthering my personal purpose, we were furthering that of the team.

In my experience, purpose-led businesses achieve real, meaningful success. Purposeful teams win in a manner that lays down the foundations for future success. Purpose-led players, employees and people can derive greater motivation to not only deliver success, but to *continue to deliver it*. To go from great to great, as we would say in sport. That's why purpose lies at the heart of the Art of Winning, a higher calling that benefits both the collective good and the individual.

During my period of repurposing when I retired from rugby, I was introduced to Tim Brown, a former New Zealand international football player who, with Joey Zwillinger, an engineer and renewables expert, founded the footwear brand Allbirds in 2016. Tim's journey is of particular interest to me, as he is a former professional sportsman who has gone on to have huge success in business. When he retired from football in 2012, Tim was so driven about achieving during his next chapter that when he launched Allbirds he was determined to become better known for being the co-founder of Allbirds – for what he is doing *now* – than as an ex-professional footballer.

Allbirds has since been valued at over a billion dollars, has stores all over the world and was listed on the Nasdaq in 2021. I think it's fair to say he's achieved his goal, which strikes me as a major achievement.

What really makes Allbirds stand out, however, is its strong sense of purpose. The company's core mantra is 'create better things in a better way', which means putting sustainability at the heart of its business. Allbirds is a certified B Corporation – a measure of a company's social and environmental performance – and its purpose runs through everything it does, from the sustainable wool fabric it uses to the carbon footprint it shares with each pair of its shoes (the ambition is to one day reach net zero – a metric along the road to striving towards its purpose).

But sustainability alone isn't enough. As Tim says, 'People don't buy sustainable products. They buy great ones. We can make great products that are sustainable.' And this marriage of quality and sustainability, powered by a strong purpose, has allowed Allbirds to create innovations like a natural, carbon-negative type of EVA (ethylene-vinyl acetate) – a common synthetic material in footwear derived from fossil fuels. But not only this, because of its powerful environmental-driven purpose – the higher calling beyond simply selling units or winning games – it made this innovation open-source, so that other like-minded companies could use it, and create a bigger environmental impact as a result. And by following this purpose, there were then profit-driven benefits to this decision: with more companies using such a material, it means the cost of it comes down.

So, for companies like Allbirds, the strong purpose it is striving towards is driving profit, success and innovation along the way. It is a company working towards something far bigger than itself – something far bigger than any one of us. There's no finish line to its purpose, no flag to be planted at the end.

If I look back now on my own career and ask of our own purpose, *Were we the most dominant team in the history of world rugby?* I don't know – probably not. But we did achieve some amazing things and I would hope we'd at least be part of any debate around that subject. I will still find myself on occasion asking, *What would an All Black great do?* And even now, with my boots well and truly hung up, I know that it's a question that will lead me to the right decision – one that puts the good of the team first.

THREE POINTS - PURPOSE

With the All Blacks the coaches would brief the key players in the leadership group on the game plan and tactics, and it would be our responsibility as the leaders of each of our respective sections – in my case the attacking strategy – to deliver the main 'headlines' in clear, precise and direct language so that it stuck in players' heads. You don't want to be overcomplicating these things close to a game. In that spirit I will provide three 'headline' points at the end of each chapter. By the end of the book, you will have thirty points – and, as any player will attest, if you finish a match with that many you're doing something right.

1. Your purpose is bigger than a goal – it must aspire to something bigger than yourself and have no end point, so that you're always striving towards it.

2. A personal purpose and the team's collective purpose need to be a perfect partnership – there's no room for division on this journey.

3. A purpose points the way, but only through breaking it down into manageable pieces, asking *how* you will achieve it, can you hope to walk towards it.

A culture needs to absorb the legacy of those that have gone before, and yet also point towards the future.

CHAPTER 2

WHAKAPAPA

I come from a long line of rugby-playing people from both sides of my family. My middle name is William, after Bill Dalley, my mum's great-uncle, who was not only an All Black, but a member of The Invincibles, the legendary New Zealand side that won every game on their tour of 1924–5.

Dad's dad, Granddad Carter, had five sons, who all played rugby competitively. Dad's fond of telling a story about the time when Southbridge put out a side with four Carters in the back line – him and three of his brothers – and the fact is that my dad played something like 300 games for Southbridge until he was in his forties, alongside working full-time as a builder. He's coached players at the club – including me – and to this day is still heavily involved in Southbridge as a life member.

When I was talking to my dad during the writing of this book, I realised just how similar our respective childhoods were: a generation apart, we spent all our spare time at the club, doing odd jobs and helping out around the club in return for a Moro bar or a can of Coke, in my case, or a popsicle for him.

I'm simply the latest in a long line of rugby-playing ancestors, and it will be up to my sons and future generations in the family to continue that line, should they choose to.

Within the All Blacks, we formed part of a long line of teams going back all the way to The Originals team that toured the British Isles in 1905, and moving forward through The Invincibles team, the 1987 inaugural World Cup winners and the 1996 team, who were the first to win a tour of South Africa. After I, and several of my long-serving teammates, retired from the All Blacks following the 2015 World Cup final, other All Blacks teams followed and will continue to follow, each creating their own legacy and learning from that of those who came before them.

And even within that, I belong to a long line of All Black number 10s, players I've admired and been inspired by, who have all made their own mark upon that jersey, just as I in turn made mine upon it and passed it on to the next player to wear it.

So why the history lesson? Well, when looking at the culture of any organisation, it is vital that a leader looks first to the past to establish the core values and derive strength and direction, just as any individual deciding where they walk next should first look at where they've walked from. When you start to learn about your past, it gives you the motivation to continue and enhance that legacy.

In New Zealand we call this whakapapa, and it became a vital element in the evolution of the culture of the All Blacks.

LEVERAGING YOUR PAST

In 2004, following a poor Tri Nations series, it became very clear that big changes to our culture were needed. Our relatively new All Blacks coaching team of Graham Henry, Steve Hansen and Wayne Smith had decided they'd had enough. Wayne Smith in particular was on the verge of quitting because this wasn't an All Blacks culture he could be proud of. There were too many hangovers from the amateur days, and something more profound than just a change of team selection or tactics was required. It was time to tackle systemic, cultural issues to create a new All Blacks environment more befitting of the high-performance professional era and the twenty-first century.

Having said that, of course, team selection *did* play a part in it too: in November's northern hemisphere tour of that year some familiar faces were missing, and instead a more youthful side was picked, along with the return of some players who had thought their All Black career was behind them. It was a bold move from the coaches to put such faith in youth, and it was the first time I would play number 10 for the All Blacks, at the age of twenty-two – another bold move by them, when you consider the experienced players I would be replacing. This would form my first experience in a leadership role within the All Blacks: running the back line and becoming part of the decision-making process in the team.

Indeed, the players would play a major role in this great cultural shift. Tana Umaga, whom Graham Henry had made his captain earlier in the year, and Richie McCaw, already a natural leader at that time, really got hold of the culture along with the coaches and created profound changes that would be felt for years to come. Things like **No one is bigger than the team** and the environment of excellence were already very much a part of the culture, but newer emphasis on cultural aspects like **Better people make better All Blacks** – or 'no dickheads', if you prefer – and the idea that **The players drive the team** instead of the coaches came out of this process.

These cultural touchstones will be explored throughout this book and are among the key ingredients to the Art of Winning. But, arguably, the defining change that would embody our culture throughout our time with the All Blacks was made palpable the following year, in 2005, before the home series against the British and Irish Lions.

Before the start of the Lions tour each of us was presented with an All Blacks book. Within its pages was an exploration of the history of the All Blacks. The unique, special, multicultural teams I mentioned at the start of this chapter featured, along with information about all of the tournaments and competitions we would play in – the World Cups, Tri Nations, the Bledisloe Cup, the Hillary Shield.

This was the physical manifestation of what we'd been trying to do since the previous year, to *look back* at where we'd come from, at all the teams who had gone before us. There was great strength to be gleaned from learning about this – about appreciating the fact that we were simply the latest in a long line of All Blacks, that we were mere custodians of the jersey. Through leveraging our past we were able to see the standards that were demanded of us, that it was our responsibility to do right by our ancestors. Who wants to be the weak link in a chain that goes back over a century? We had levels that not only had to be maintained – but improved upon, as our purpose within this team was *to leave the jersey in a better place than when we found it.*

It's a powerful task for any organisation with a history to look back and examine what the past can teach and inspire in us. A culture needs to absorb the legacy of those that have gone before, and yet also point towards the future. For some organisations, this might mean looking back through a past that features a significant setback or something negative – a scandal or wrong turn, or period of poor performance, for example – during its history. The challenge then becomes to delve beyond this to find something positive that you can be proud to continue and build on. The answer may lie in how the organisation recovered from these setbacks or, if you're in the process of doing the recovering, in the organisation's past before the setback. Even if you need to change radically at that moment, it's not about patting yourself on the back or ignoring problems, but instead finding something in the legacy of those who went before you that can inspire you and your people.

In his book *Belonging*, Owen Eastwood (Ngāi Tahu), who has worked with the cultures in the South Africa cricket team and England football team among others, describes whakapapa as:

Each of us is part of an unbreakable chain of people going back and forward in time. Back to our first

*ancestor at the beginning of time and into the future
to the end of time.*

And it is this future that was the foundation of the second part of the All Blacks book. After the information about the tournaments and what had come before us, the back of the book consisted of a lot of blank pages. These were for us to write our own legacy into.

For the rest of my All Black career, anyone who played their first Test match would get an All Blacks book. It became a powerful symbol of just how special it was to be in that culture, and it became a rite of passage for induction into the All Blacks tribe. A powerful ritual that looked back to the All Blacks before us, while looking forward to those who would follow us. Receiving it served as a ceremony that affirmed our core value: *Each and every player is merely a custodian of the jersey, making the most of their time before they hand the jersey on – in a stronger position than when they received it. The job of anyone receiving the jersey is simply to **enhance the legacy**.*

A NEW SPIN ON THE OLD THING

Looking to the past and learning why we were there helped foster a great sense of *belonging* in the environment. It made you feel grateful for the opportunity to be part of it and appreciate just how short it was, this time as a custodian of the jersey. Just as with a strong purpose, it allowed us to feel we were part of something far bigger than simply a team trying to win its next match or tournament (although we obviously wanted to do that as well). We were striving to enhance the legacy of our ancestors, many of whom were around before we were even born, and to play our part on the stage of something that would continue long after we'd hung up our boots (and even after we die). And most importantly, we were all in it together.

It's important to stress that looking back in such a way isn't the same as directly repeating what came before or becoming a slave to the past. If anything, it's quite the opposite: it's about respecting and recognising where you've come from, and being empowered by it. And this empowerment that we took from our collective desire to enhance the legacy of the team led to all sorts of new things happening within the environment, driven by the players.

This philosophy led to us looking at perhaps the most sacred ritual of all associated with the All Blacks: the haka. We looked back at the haka through time and specifically 'Ka Mate', the predominant haka used for as far back as we could remember, and thought about how we could enhance it and make it more relevant to the new culture we were creating. It took a lot of hard work and time to bring to life, as well as consultation with the right experts in the area, but the result was 'Kapa o Pango', which we debuted in August 2005, against South Africa.

A new haka for a renewed culture. We were leveraging our past to build our future. But the way we went about it offers a lesson to any culture or organisation that wants to create a fresh spin on what they do. We took something that was core to the essence of the All Blacks, something sacred, and we put our own perspective on it. But we could only do it through studying and understanding the haka's history and its cultural significance, and being respectful and sympathetic to that, just as any institution making cultural change must understand its own history and remain true to that.

It was a very special moment indeed for me in November 2013, before we played England at Twickenham, which was to be my hundredth Test match for the All Blacks. During the 'Kapa o Pango' haka led by Liam Messam, he slapped my back and pulled me up by my shirt as a tribute to my All Black career. It was an incredible gesture to receive from a teammate and it was a moment that demonstrated to me the power of the culture we had created. Here we were performing our sacred pre-match ritual, the haka, in a form that we had created ourselves, while also marking the occasion of my own legacy of reaching a hundred matches and enjoying a tribute from one of my teammates in a show of togetherness. Just as with our purpose, the individual and the collective were aligned, and this idea of a higher calling beyond simply winning the game was palpable.

_____

CORE VALUES

The All Blacks book was the physical symbol of our team's whakapapa, and it was this looking back that allowed us to fully focus on what we believed to be the core values of the All

Blacks, and how we could best implement these values to strengthen our culture and our future. You see this in the best organisations from all walks of life – from business and charities to sport and media. Great organisations know how to use their legacy and remain faithful to it while still being able to evolve and grow.

Businesses with a long, grand history such as Louis Vuitton are able to use their legacy of travel, craftsmanship and *savoir faire* that its consumers are familiar with, going back to its roots as a nineteenth-century trunk maker, and put a new perspective on it, such as their aptly titled Core Values campaign in which they used travel in the sense of an emotional journey to promote their luxury goods. And yet it isn't necessary to have such a long history: the cycling clothing brand Rapha, for example, is a solely twenty-first-century company that has built up values of quality, passion for its sport and crucially a social aspect – of *doing* this sport rather than simply selling things for it – through its cycling clubs across the world in a short period of time, building a genuine and invested community around its brand. Its mission – or its poetry – is 'to make road cycling the most popular sport in the world', which cuts through everything they do, just as enhancing the legacy was at the heart of everything we did in the All Blacks.

When I finished playing and began my process of repurposing, with the help of Kevin Roberts I first looked back at my own playing career, my whakapapa, and then tried to establish the core values I had built up throughout my years of playing rugby. I was effectively asking myself, *Who am I?*

It's an incredibly confrontational and conflicting process to actually sit down and answer that question clearly. To ask myself, *Who is Dan Carter?* With Kevin's help we examined my character and tried to distil what my values are. And Kevin wouldn't let me get away with wishy-washy answers: he wanted to help me get to the core of it all before I could explore my purpose. (We'll look at how you can address your own core values at the end of this section.)

I had to look back unflinchingly at my whole career, the soaring highs and the brutal lows, and hold a magnifying glass up to my deep-rooted beliefs and values, look at where I've walked *from*, so that I could establish where I needed to walk to. Only through establishing these core values, intrinsic to anything I do in life, could I then begin to look more confidently at where my future might lie.

It was a process that forced me to face up to some of my insecurities, particularly about my education, my lack of a university degree and some of the moments I could have handled a lot better, but it also freed me of some of them. I might not have a degree in my back pocket, but I have had another kind of education that has value in the world outside of rugby. And I have values that I must remain true to in this next chapter of my life if I am to achieve any kind of success and satisfaction.

Facing up to this self-doubt reminded me of a technique I used as a rugby player, when I would measure success through the number of consecutive kicks I made during training sessions. When I get a string of eighteen or nineteen consecutive kicks between the posts, my self-belief is through the roof. But if I miss three in a row, doubt creeps in – about myself and my technique. All of a sudden, I'm thinking, *I just need one. Just one successful kick.* And often, if I'm having a shocker, I'll bring it back to a readily attainable goal – I'll put the ball on the tee in a really easy position. I'll take the kick and think, *OK, I've got that right now.* And then I'll do it again. And again. *OK, getting a bit more self-belief here.* And then I'll start moving it around to more challenging positions, and before I know it, I'm back on a streak of consecutive kicks.

One way to overcome self-doubt involves bringing yourself back to short-term milestones. Set yourself small, achievable goals, and then things can snowball from there and self-belief can build. The doubts about my education, for example, were mitigated by achieving smaller goals that provided evidence that I had much to offer despite my lack of formal education, and which snowballed from there into self-belief: the opportunities to speak with AstraZeneca, the Nuffield Department of Surgical Sciences and Louis Vuitton, which I mentioned at the beginning of this book, were part of that, and as I overcame this self-doubt and started to build some self-belief, I felt confident enough to reach a little further – such as by writing this book that you hold now.

Just as, similarly, you might harbour some self-doubt about ever achieving the career path you're on. But by setting those small, achievable goals, you can start to provide the evidence that disputes this self-doubt. That might mean setting a goal to polish your CV and apply for jobs, or that training course that will put you on the right path towards your purpose; or asking for some robust, practical feedback from people whose opinion you respect. Clear, easy-to-achieve goals. And then you might get an interview, maybe several – your confidence builds – and then you get the right job, you do well at it, progress rapidly – your self-belief skyrockets.

Ultimately, a lot of self-doubt derives from too great a focus on the outcome, rather than the process that goes into creating that outcome, something we'll explore in more depth in Chapter 4 (Mind Management). But for now, suffice to say, you have to have a process to turn to when self-doubt creeps in, and it all comes back to the work. You need to do the work. The preparation is ultimately where I derived most of my self-belief as a player, and it was also the source of our collective self-belief as a team. When you do the work, you have the confidence to know you've done everything to give yourself the best chance of performing to the best of your abilities – and the outcome takes care of itself.

Finding your core values isn't easy. You might initially struggle to think of any. Or you might find that you come up with lots of words that, on closer inspection, don't mean an awful lot to you. With Kevin's guidance, I attached a number to the values I came up with and ranked them, and you could do this with your own, putting them into order of importance. Because you need to find a way of filtering them down to the ones that cut to the heart of who you are and will help you moving forward. It might be that you only settle on two or three things that you really care about, but that's better than not having any at all. Because when things aren't going well or you're not performing, they're a benchmark to return to and to ask yourself, 'Are we living these values? Or are we falling short?' Along with your purpose, it's a constant reminder of where you want to be heading. And if we return to whakapapa once again, it's vital to understand that this future is as important as the past.

WHAT ARE YOUR CORE VALUES?

Can you confront your own past and develop your own? Some useful questions to help guide you include:

- What are my red lines – what would I *never* do?

- What are my beliefs?

- What drives me?

- What defines me: what three positive words would you use to describe yourself?

- Where have I come from? And where am I going?

- What do you love about your past that you want to take forward into your future?

Attach a numerical value to each of the core beliefs you come up with – it could be as simple as ranking them 1–10 – so that you can assign meaningful values that are clear to you and your purpose. It's better to have two or three strong values than ten weaker ones that don't really mean a great deal to you.

SUCCESSION

After the 2015 Rugby World Cup final, a number of long-standing players had played their last game for the All Blacks. Ma'a Nonu and I were going to play in France the following season, Richie McCaw and Keven Mealamu were retiring. Tony Woodcock had played his last game for the All Blacks earlier in the competition, in the final pool game against Tonga, in which he was injured, and his competition ended prematurely. Each of these players, including me, had more than a hundred caps. Conrad Smith, who had a mere ninety-four caps, had also donned the All Black jersey for the last time and was going to play in France.

If you look at the loss of experience, leadership and class in that squad, it would be natural to assume there'd be some kind of drop-off in performance after the World Cup win, certainly a good period of restructuring to come. After all, it often happens with teams who win a World Cup, let alone one in which six vastly experienced players leave the set-up immediately afterwards as well. It would have been easy for the 2016 team to have a poor year. But that wasn't what happened at all.

Instead, the All Blacks had a fantastic 2016, winning all three of their games against Wales in the June internationals and winning the Rugby Championship with two games to spare. It even surprised me just how good they were, but this seamless transition didn't happen by accident.

We'd been living our purpose to be the most dominant team in the history of world rugby for some time by 2015.

Living those values, day by day. Challenging anyone who failed to meet the standards required. We were guided by that purpose fully in the knowledge that we wouldn't necessarily be around to see it through to its conclusion; that it was a mission that would go beyond the end of many of our careers was inherent in the purpose of the All Blacks team.

This married perfectly with the work we had done looking back at the legacy of the All Blacks who had come before us, empowering us to leave the jersey in a better place. That didn't just mean leaving a legacy of dazzling silverware for the next generation to aspire to; it meant empowering them and enabling them to sustain the success we had achieved, so that they in turn could leave the jersey in a better place.

We had planned for the moment when we would all retire. We had been building towards that day. The work that our three coaches had done in getting the players to drive the culture meant that we had a leadership group in place to do just that – a subject we will return to in more detail later in the book – and we created a 'future leadership group' with players like Beauden Barrett, Brodie Retallick and Sam Cane brought into our leadership group and upskilled so that when we left, their leadership journey didn't start that day. It had been going on for years. Kieran Read, who would be made captain after the World Cup, was a big part of the transition and had been working alongside Richie for years.

In a culture like ours the sudden drop-off predicted after the World Cup just isn't going to happen. Our purpose and our culture had driven home our responsibility to the next generation because we knew we were part of something much bigger, not only than ourselves, but even than the team we were play-ing in. To quote Owen Eastwood one more time, we were part of that 'unbreakable chain of people going back and forward in time. Back to our first ancestor at the beginning of time and into the future to the end of time.' We owed it to those who had come before and to those who would come after to ensure that our team, our tribe, to which we belonged, would remain at the top even after we had gone.

The pressure I put myself under was always far greater than anything the media or opposition or fans could muster, and in the same way the standards we aspire to as All Blacks are far greater than anything the opponents, fans or media set for us. We live by the standards and demands made by our ancestors. We are trying to measure ourselves by them, the toughest yard-stick of all, rather than any of our opponents.

ARE YOU UPSKILLING THE FUTURE LEADERS IN YOUR ORGANISATION?

A rugby team has only one captain, but there are many leaders in the team, just as a high-performance organi-sation in any field must have leaders throughout. Who knows what tomorrow might bring: people move on to other opportunities, market forces are subject to change, takeovers and mergers do happen, and retirement might come for senior leaders (at a more appropriate age than in professional rugby, of course). If your organisation lost a couple of key people at once, is your succession planning robust enough to ensure continued success? You just need to take a look at the managerial merry-go-round in professional club football to see examples of poor succession planning. Whereas Graham Henry was the All Blacks head coach for seven years (and two World Cups) before his successor Steve Hansen was promoted from within the set-up to become head coach for the next two World Cups.

In business, the best companies have succession at the forefront of their planning, and just like the All Blacks, they often have their future leaders already in their ranks, living and breathing the culture and developing as a leader within the environment before they move up, so that the transition is seamless. Tim Cook has been the CEO of Apple since 2011. He was groomed for several years to be the successor to Steve Jobs, just as he is now grooming his own successors. As Cook put it in an interview with BuzzFeed News in 2017: 'I see my role as CEO to prepare as many people as I can to be CEO.' In a culture like Apple's, he can see that part of his role is to prepare the company for life after him. Cook is a custodian of the proverbial jersey who has overseen huge growth at Apple, continuing the success of the company founded and led by Jobs. He will pass his jersey on to the next CEO, who will have all the tools to continue Apple's success long after he is gone.

FIND WHAT YOU LOVE ABOUT YOUR PAST AND BUILD IT INTO YOUR FUTURE

During the captain's run before the first Test against the British and Irish Lions in 2005 in Christchurch, I'd decided I wanted a piece of the grass from the Lancaster Park stadium. This was my home ground, where I had spent so much of my youth on the embankment watching the team – and now I was here on the grass on the biggest stage, against a team that only toured New Zealand once every twelve years.

I taped that turf to the first blank page at the end of my All Blacks book, the section in which we leave our own legacy, and on the morning of the match I first wrote down how I was feeling – I'd always start with that – and then I wrote down a few pre-game notes to myself. This is what I wrote:

> *I'm shitting myself.*
> *Very nervous.*
> *Playing with a team of champions vs the best team I've ever played.*
> *Preparation done.*
> *Just back my instincts and be positive.*

For the next match, the second Test against the Lions, I wrote down a few notes to myself again:

> *Starting to get very nervous.*
> *Nothing to lose.*

Need to leave it all out there.
Go nuts.
Work all day.
Back yourself, always!

As you can see, even before the match of my life, I was clearly nervous, something we'll explore in more depth in Chapter 5 (Pressure Is a Privilege). And these pre-game notes weren't detailed instructions or preparation, they weren't the ten moves we were playing, the game plan or the kicking strategy: that work had all been done in my other book. This was simply how I felt and some trigger words for me to write down on the morning of the game. *The work is done, now what do I want to have in my head as I go into the match?*

The most important use of that book for me, however, was as a reminder of why I was there. The book was always with me, no matter where I was in the world, and at the start of each season or campaign I would flick through the pages and just take in the significance of what we were doing, the footprints I was walking in – and the footprints I hoped to leave behind.

Leading up to the 2015 World Cup, ten years later, the All Blacks book was about to be updated. There was much to fill it with, of course: including that Lions series in 2005, three Grand Slam tours – in which we beat all four of the home nations, England, Ireland, Scotland and Wales – in 2005, 2008 and 2010, and of course the World Cup in 2011. I was honoured to be asked to write a section for the book, about the Lions series in 2005. In a sense, this was an opportunity to leave my legacy in writing, to talk about that once-in-a-career series that featured arguably my best game in the black jersey as part of a formidable team performance. They still give out the All Blacks books to this day, and it's a source of pride to have my – our – legacy as a member of the All Blacks immortalised in print – to have laid down my footprints in ink.

After my first season for Kobe Steelers in Japan, I returned home to my family in New Zealand for a ten-month break in 2019. Japan was hosting the Rugby World Cup later in the year, and the Top League season wouldn't commence until after the World Cup. This was my first time away from the game since my sabbatical in 2014, when I took time off to rebuild my body. It was my first taste of what life was going to be like when I finished playing – a window into a world without rugby.

This gave me the opportunity to identify the things I was most going to miss about the game and see how I could find a way of integrating them into my post-rugby life. It gave me the chance to explore what I loved about my past so that I could build it into my future.

The camaraderie, the banter of the dressing room, teammates pushing each other to ever greater heights: I knew this was something that I would miss and feel keenly. For anyone retiring from sport fortunate not to be managing any significant physical or mental injury, this is possibly the hardest one. You're just not going to be able to recreate that feeling in a meeting room working for a business.

So, this is how the Glory Days was born. A group of ex-players such as Ali Williams, Doug Howlett, Leon MacDonald and I would meet up, train, play golf and have some fun at our own expense now that we were 'has-beens'. And the Glory

Days definitely filled that void for us, because the social side of the game is so important. It can feel lonely when that's taken away, when you're no longer part of that unit working towards a game each weekend.

The other thing I knew I was going to miss was that buzz and the butterflies that come from striving towards great things. During my period of repurposing following retirement, I happened to holiday in the same part of New Zealand as John Brakenridge, who was CEO of The New Zealand Merino Company for twenty-seven years and is credited as playing a huge role in transforming the fortunes of New Zealand's merino industry and making it the luxury product it is today. John paid tribute to my rugby career and then said, 'You can have a similar level of impact on this next stage of your life, but what type of impact do you want to make on the world? It could be social, environmental, economic impact.'

What this question crystallised for me was that social impact would have to be at the heart of what came next for me. With the work I'd already done with Kevin Roberts, looking back at my past and exploring what my values were, I knew that it wasn't the trophies or the individual awards that I was most proud of. It was the impact I'd been able to have on the next generation. I thought back once again to the players who had inspired me growing up, and this idea that I was continuing that legacy. And this is what has led me to mentor some young athletes, to partner with UNICEF to help support children in need, and to work with the Oxford Foundry to share my knowledge and experience with the next generation of leaders.

Because what I was doing here is *finding what I love about my past and building it into my future*. It was only through looking back and examining where I'd come from that I could see in what direction I wanted to go next. And it's a process any individual or organisation must undertake when they're going through a period of change, whether that's repurposing, a cultural reset or a response to a drastic change in circumstances. It's certainly the process we went through as part of our cultural evolution with the All Blacks in 2004, just as any business that hopes to endure must find what works from its own past and build it into its future in some form.

What's crucial to this, however, is the commitment to it from your people. Through being a custodian of the jersey, we had a very real stake in the All Blacks – it made us feel like co-owners in a company whose future we had a strong investment in beyond our own playing career. The challenge in a business environment, where profit and loss stand in for wins and losses, is to try to replicate this feeling. For companies just starting out, the ambition must surely be to reach a point when enough history has been built to draw upon and create these strong narratives to inspire this feeling. And for longer-standing companies, the objective is to draw out what is inspiring and purposeful about your past, to adapt it so that it's relevant and effective and then to make it an integral part of your identity, one that both your people and your customers can buy into.

THREE POINTS - WHAKAPAPA

1. Just like a superhero, everyone has an origin story: find yours. Before you walk forward, first look back to see where you've come from.

2. What are your key values? How can you ensure these values become enshrined in your work, your team, your community or your organisation?

3. Leave the jersey in a better place: what is the legacy you want to leave behind?

Everyone in the organisation needs to be moving in the right direction together, and it only takes one person moving the other way to disrupt the harmony and threaten a culture.

CHAPTER 3

HUMILITY

NO INDIVIDUAL IS BIGGER THAN THE TEAM

In 2014, some ten years after the beginnings of the cultural evolution instigated by Henry, Hansen and Smith, with Steve Hansen now our head coach, we played against the USA at Soldier Field in Chicago, home stadium of their NFL team the Bears. It was a watershed occasion for a couple of reasons: firstly because it was the first rugby Test match ever to be played at an NFL stadium, with more than 60,000 people in attendance; and secondly – and more personally – because it was my first Test match for almost a year.

I came off the bench in the second half and played well, kicking three out of three conversions and feeling good. I came off the field feeling that I was in for a great end to the tour. *Sometimes you can just feel it.* I sat out the next game against England, but I started the following one against Scotland. And, in that match, I had one of my worst games ever in the jersey. *Sometimes those feelings are just wrong.*

So, after I get the knock at my hotel door and find one of the coaches telling me that they want to have a word, and they let me know that I would not be playing the next match against Wales, I'm upset. I'm down. I want to know why.

They explain that Beauden Barrett (Beaudy) and Aaron Cruden (Crudes) are the top two number 10s at this stage. Does that make me third choice? Or, given that Colin Slade will be on the bench ahead of me, *fourth* choice?

'We feel the in-form player is Beaudy,' they say, 'and he'll start against Wales.'

I'm gutted. Devastated, even, having just got myself back into contention after my *annus horribilis* of injuries and feeling in a very down and dark place. But at the same time there's something else there, a feeling that's just a seed at first, and then, once that initial disappointment begins to settle, once the anger subsides, the seed grows and becomes something more certain: the feeling that it is **the best decision for the team**.

Players like Beaudy and Crudes have been playing and guiding the team all season, after all, and crucially in an environment of excellence such as ours, we trust the decision of the coaches, we have implicit faith in the culture and environment. I'm not bigger than the team.

So, what can I do next? Selfishly, I could just drop my lip and hope they have a bad game, but that's not befitting of the environment. That's not the sort of thing that is going to enhance the legacy of the jersey. Instead, I contribute at meetings. I share my knowledge with the players in my position. And when I get the opportunity, I make the most of it.

Because in this environment, **no individual is bigger than the team**. We are all striving towards the greater good. And while it's one thing in any organisation to say words to that effect, it's quite another to create the sort of environment and culture where this value becomes implicit, second nature to your people. That requires time and, crucially, trust.

THE BACKBONE

No individual is bigger than the team was always an All Black value. In fact, I would say it's a Kiwi value too. It's how we are as people. We tend to put others first – it's in our DNA. It's always been a part of being an All Black, but I would say now that there were signs early in my career that it wasn't as big a focus as it could have been.

When I first came into the All Blacks environment in 2003, I was playing number 12 (inside centre). It was a World Cup year and I knew that there were better players in front of me – the likes of Aaron Mauger and Ma'a Nonu – and then at number 10 there were players like Carlos Spencer and Andrew Mehrtens. When I wasn't playing, which was usual, I knew I could relax – though that's not to say I wasn't disappointed not to be involved.

Often if you didn't get picked back then, the players who missed out would go out on the Thursday before the match for dinner and have a few beers to get over the disappointment – maybe let off some steam. We were known as the DDs – the 'Dirty Dirties' – which basically meant we had no value to the team for the rest of the week from Thursday onwards. Our responsibilities would include doing our gym work and taking on the lion's share of the sponsorship and media duties, and not a lot else. The twenty-three members of the squad need to focus on the game, went the logic, so it was up to us to take the sponsorship and media on. There was clear separation between those who were playing and those who were not.

I remember before one Test match, against South Africa in Christchurch, our winger Joe Rokocoko wasn't selected for the team – he was in the DDs. He trained on Friday, as the DDs did, and then on Saturday morning did a big gym session – heavy squats and all. But then in the warm-up our winger Sitiveni Sivivatu went down. All of a sudden, Joe Rokocoko had to play after one of the worst twenty-four hours of preparation you could possibly do prior to a Test match. Thankfully Joe Rokocoko is a bit of a freak of an athlete and had a fantastic game, but that was a bit of a wake-up call. *We all need to prepare to play.*

Things have changed a lot since then. Now, we no longer have the DDs. We call these players the *backbone* of the team. We no longer prepare any differently whether we're playing or not, which means all the players do the sponsorship and media duties. The DDs no longer go out to let off steam on Thursday: how about we work together, and *all* enjoy a drink together after the Test match?

What that does is create a more inclusive environment in which everyone feels that they offer value, and it gives the squad more flexibility should the unexpected happen. It offers cultural cohesion and, crucially, creates a more competitive environment. The members of the backbone would train as hard as anyone in the team and would be given more owner-ship, more skin in the game. If, for example, we were preparing to play Australia, then the backbone would take on the role of the Australians in training, running their plays. The coaches loved to see the backbone fully commit to these roles, and the added incentive for the players was that if you were perform-ing well in this environment, it meant you were potentially gunning for that jersey.

By this time, if you weren't privy to the information, you wouldn't be able to tell the difference between those who were playing and those who weren't right up until kick-off. We all prepared the same way, as one. The players in the team would go out and play, and then after the game, the players who didn't play would do their top-up work, as they were fresher. What they didn't do was get stuck into their top-up work and heavy squats on the morning of the match.

DO YOU HAVE A BACKBONE, OR DOES YOUR ORGANISATION HAVE THE 'DIRTY DIRTIES' MENTALITY?

In any team you have what might be described as the 'first-team players', the people who do the front-line work, get the most exposure and attention and, when it comes to it, the glory. But just like a sports team, every organisation will also have the squad players on the bench – the support and administrative staff who don't get the same amount of attention as those first-team players. Making sure these support staff are treated fairly, inclusively and equally with the first-team players will help foster a far greater sense of being part of a team, and offers competitive advantages such as these people being more able and confident of stepping up and contributing when needed – and crucially being more willing to. It can be a demoralising place to be, the 'Dirty Dirties'. But things will feel much different as part of a crucial backbone.

RECRUIT ON CHARACTER

When you're building a culture in any organisation, it has to be driven by the people. There's no point having just the managers and coaches espousing the values and then expecting the culture to grow and thrive. Your people have to buy into the purpose, the desire to enhance the legacy – and then they ultimately have to drive the culture, the idea that no individual is bigger than the team. It's an incredibly powerful thing to have a collective aligned in this mindset, all pushing in the same direction, living the values and speaking up when they see they're not being met.

There are two approaches, both of which are necessary in tandem to achieve the right blend of people to drive the culture. Firstly, you have to recruit on character, not just talent. If you have the choice between an absolute superstar who is gunning for individual glory or a harder-working, better cultural fit, it's not difficult to work out who is going to last longer in a high-performance environment. When Graham Henry and his

74

team pressed the reset button in 2004, it was with the idea of driving this new culture that younger players were promoted and those who had been out in the cold for some time were selected. One of the clearest changes I saw during my time with the All Blacks was this transition to selecting players that could add to the culture, that could be relied upon not to bring too much of an ego and live the value that the team is the most important thing.

It's a theme that is of equal importance in the world of start-ups. Reid Hoffman told me, 'Not every A player should work for your company. You only really define your culture well when [you have] an A player who would fit with you but not with someone else, or would fit with someone else and not you.' As Reid puts it, you're looking for people who can align with the way your organisation plays the game.

This isn't just about the A players, though. You need *everyone* aligned to play the game your way, from the most junior in an organisation all the way to the CEO. In order for any organisation to function to its fullest potential, everyone needs to do their role so that the next person can do theirs. If even one part of it isn't aligned, then you're not functioning at the level you're capable of.

Secondly, whether it's a business or a sports team, you need to onboard these people into the environment rapidly, immersing them in the culture: what is expected of them, what it means to be part of this team, how to stay in the environment and grow and flourish. As soon as a player joined the squad for the first time, a couple of players from the leadership group would begin onboarding them. The All Blacks book was a part of this, of course, and players like Brad Thorn and Keven Mealamu would drive their baptism into the values of the culture we were building. Culture has to be at the heart of any onboarding process.

At the same time, a high-performance culture isn't a straitjacket environment where individuality needs muting or toning down. There are so many opportunities to express yourself, to be yourself and to speak up in the All Blacks environment – which is a player-driven environment at heart. But everyone needs to understand the context, that these are the values that make this All Blacks team so great, and if you want to add to this legacy you need to live these values. And one of the most important is that the decisions you make are for the team, not just for you. If you're benefitting individually but sacrificing the success of the team, it's the wrong decision. Simple as that. Any conversation or debate needs to be resolved with this simple mantra in mind: **What's best for the team?**

KEEPING YOUR FEET ON THE GROUND

For a young and talented player, being inducted into a culture like the All Blacks can be quite challenging. They might have been the high-school hero who moved seamlessly through the academy system as one of the top players, a long and glittering career assured before them. They might have been taught about leadership, about the value of one's own opinion, and then they're so talented that they get into the All Blacks and they expect it all to just happen.

But there's a danger in getting ahead of yourself in an environment like this. This player might be the reason their school team was so successful – individual players can make such a huge difference to the outcome in age-grade rugby or at provincial level. But once you're at the very highest level, you're not going to be the sole reason why the All Blacks win or lose. The standard is far too high – you're a cog in the machine. Unless you're Jonah Lomu, of course. But even then, despite his game-changing individual brilliance, he was still a team man.

It would be the same for a talented executive in a small or medium-sized business moving to a multinational corporation – can they adapt to the scale of it? Can their ego handle their new status as a little fish in a far larger pond? Because if they can't align and swim in the same direction as the rest of the company, then it's going to cause problems. Everyone in the organisation needs to be moving in the right direction together, and it only takes one person moving the other way to disrupt the harmony and threaten a culture.

For a young player entering the environment, it can be a bit of a wake-up call to realise they're no longer the 'main man'. But it is the ones who can adjust to this transition who will flourish, and everyone coming into the environment does so with their eyes open about the expectations demanded of them. Initially, they should use the environment to listen and learn, and then very quickly be offering and giving input. Humility is at the core of this. Knowing who you are, where you're from – not getting ahead of yourself.

In 2005 I had a very good year: a fantastic series against the British and Irish Lions, I had just started playing number 10

for the All Blacks in only my third year of playing profession-
ally, and I was named World Rugby Player of the Year at the
age of only twenty-three. With that kind of success there's a
chance I could start to think I'm a bit bigger than the team,
that maybe I could begin to relate to the young player I've just
described above. And, let's be honest, as a young player it's
hard not to get carried away. Despite all of us athletes saying
we never read our own press, it's difficult not to at times. If
you've had an awful game, of course you're not going to. But
if you've just had a cracker of a game, what would be the harm
in a quick peek at social media? Or if you're at the airport,
you're filling in a bit of time and there's a newspaper there – it
would be rude not to have a little read.

Let's be clear, that's not going to help reinforce the idea that
no individual is bigger than the team. And making sure you
know you're not is so vital, the responsibility of both yourself
and the culture you're a part of. After every good game I had,
Steve Tew, the CEO of New Zealand Rugby, would come up
to me and kick my feet at the after-match reception. 'Just
checking,' he'd say. 'Just checking your feet are still on the
ground.' 'Well done, well played,' he'd be saying, 'but remem-
ber, you can't do it without your teammates.'

Buying into this ethos so that it comes naturally, so that the
team instinctively comes first, meant that when you got indi-
vidual awards it was almost embarrassing, in a way. I was
hugely proud to receive each of my World Rugby Player of the
Year awards, as they were a by-product of striving towards my
personal purpose and what I wanted to achieve as part of the
team, but I knew full well I couldn't have done it without the

people around me. If there's any player who received that award and didn't first think of their teammates, then they wouldn't last long in an All Blacks environment. They're doing it for the wrong reasons – they're doing it for themselves.

As it happens, sport and the world have a beautiful way of bringing you back down to earth. After the second Test against the Lions in 2005, one of the best performances I ever had in the black jersey, I was getting plenty of accolades, plenty of pats on the back. I didn't play the third Test because of injury, and my next match was in one of the most hostile environments I've ever played in, against South Africa, and I was hopeless. It was a huge wake-up call having big, brutal South Africans bearing down on me, probably feeding off all the attention and seeing it as their mission to take me down a peg or two. And they surely did – and not just for me, but for the whole team coming off the back of a 3–0 series win over the Lions. South Africa beat us 22–16 and made sure that there was no danger of this individual thinking he was bigger than the team. At the time, I certainly didn't enjoy it, but looking back now I feel grateful that I was brought back down to earth so forcefully and abruptly.

BETTER PEOPLE MAKE BETTER ALL BLACKS

Never forgetting where you come from is such a strong value for me. My upbringing and background in Southbridge, where qualities like humility, the importance of working hard for what you got and respect for your elders had been imprinted on me from a very early age, served as good preparation for the All Blacks environment. Allied to the fact that my rugby career up until that point hadn't always pointed towards playing in the black jersey, it meant that I entered the All Blacks environment full of gratitude for the opportunity. I wasn't a cocky little boy coming in thinking I deserved anything. I worked for everything I was given, and I understood very quickly that this was a learning process and an opportunity to grow not only as a player, but as a person. And I thrived off that.

Part of the culture that was being developed in the All Blacks was this idea that not only did better people make better All Blacks in terms of the character of the individuals being selected, but also the idea that helping us each to grow as a person would potentially create an improvement as a player. Anyone in the All Blacks environment is there for one reason first and foremost: because they're bloody good at rugby. But in the past the emphasis had been solely focused on rugby, and the human element hadn't been given the same level of attention.

That began to change when the coaches and management team asked the question, *How do we create this environment where they can grow and flourish and be themselves?* Efforts were made to understand the players, get to know them on a personal level: *What makes us happy? What makes us tick?*

For example, we began understanding that players need their family at the games each week, and all of a sudden the partners and wives were much more present around the team after the games. Whenever we were travelling overseas, the management, without us even knowing, were reaching out to our partners or getting video messages from them, wishing us luck or to let us know how much they missed us. They even employed someone whose sole job was to look after the families, so she was in constant communication with the partners and wives, giving them updates, making sure that they're happy. And if the wives and partners are happy, more often than not you've got happier players who are able to concentrate fully on their jobs.

Another example would be some of the Pacific Island boys who might be missing their families, so how do we help with that? Maybe we can have a kava night, where we can bring a little bit of their culture into our environment, to make them feel welcomed and included, and also to give the rest of us an insight into their culture and heritage.

But the biggest one was how do we grow them as individuals, rather than athletes? Because if you grow them as individuals, then they will reward you by being happy and content and wanting almost to repay the privilege of being in this culture and environment by performing the best they possibly can on the training field. It meant there would be real help and support for players who might have problems at home or with things like finances. These are issues that can really consume you and take your mind off rugby, and the management could see that being able to remove some of these barriers freed us up to flourish on the field.

A lot of people come into the All Blacks environment in their early twenties. They're young, they're still maturing and they come from all sorts of different backgrounds. A lot of them, me included, miss out on university, going straight from high school to rugby. But New Zealand Rugby had player-development managers, and all through my career they would work with players – not just All Blacks, but other levels of rugby too – on their education, finding them courses and opportunities to learn about subjects outside of rugby. We'd have access to a world-class nutritionist and be educated on looking after ourselves. As well as a players' association that really cared about our wellbeing. And the aim of it was, *How can you grow this young twenty-year-old and help him become a better, more rounded person?*

A lot of workplaces are now putting a huge emphasis on their employees and offering opportunities outside of their jobs and wellbeing programmes, but it's something we've been doing for the last twenty years to enable us to thrive in this environment of high performance and pressure, knowing that we've got the support and we can just go out and do what we love, which is play rugby.

SWEEP THE SHEDS

'Sweep the sheds' is one of those mantras that has become ingrained in All Blacks folklore, a simple yet pivotal corner-stone of our culture that turns it from a merely good one to a great one. I always laugh when I hear it mentioned because it's an example that's been made such a big deal of. To us, it's just something we've always done, of course, but it's funny to hear it talked about as being the difference between a good culture and a bad one: 'Ah, if we want a culture like the All Blacks then we have to sweep the sheds.'

We actually sweep the sheds because we want to. We've always done it. It's a respect thing. It's not because Steve Hansen is shouting, 'Come on, guys, sweep the sheds!' It's the players that are really driving the environment.

A lot of it comes down to discipline: if you're disciplined off the field – picking up rubbish from the team room, being on time, clearing stuff up after you've been in the changing room – then that translates to the field. You'll be disciplined there. Some weeks, when the players' discipline is off, we're late to meetings; the attitude's not quite there, it's lazy; the changing rooms are messy, drink bottles being thrown on the floor instead of the bin. And that means our performance will suffer come the weekend, because *everything* suffers when some of us aren't pulling our weight. It's the little things that can help your discipline on the field.

It's also driven by humility: *Who are we to think we should be making a mess?* When we walk into the changing room at Twickenham, it's spotless. Someone has clearly got it perfectly prepared for us, so who are we to think we can come in, do the business and then leave it a mess and expect someone else to clean it up? That's not fair; it's not who we are as human beings nor All Blacks.

One of the strengths of what we do is that it's not the guy who doesn't play who sweeps the sheds, or the young players. It's just the first person who grabs the broom, and often that was a Richie McCaw or a Steve Hansen – because **no individual is bigger than the team.** Why should they not? If you see a mess, you clean it up. It's as simple as that. It sets an amazing example for the young players coming through. The high-school hero we described earlier is sitting there seeing the captain or coach sweeping the sheds, and something resonates with them. They store it up and pass it on to the next generation.

No one should consider themselves above doing the little things that help set the standards, which is as true in a business environment as a sports one. If you have people in your organisation who don't think twice about leaving the meeting room in a mess, who see themselves as being 'above' such menial things that can in fact be the foundation of a strong culture, you might find that what start as small infringements of discipline and standards snowballs into bigger ones.

Having your people drive the culture means your people also have to police it, and that's how it worked. We'd discipline our teammates. The team room might be left a mess, drink bottles and other detritus everywhere, and the players would call each other out. It could get confrontational at times, but it's a necessary part of our culture and everyone had to play their part. Keven Mealamu is the nicest, sweetest, most caring, quietly spoken All Black I've ever played with, but he would be the guy at the front of the bus on the microphone telling the players to sort out the team room, saying it wasn't acceptable to leave it messy. 'That's not the All Blacks way,' he'd say. 'Pick up your standards.'

I have noticed this philosophy in other high-performance environments more recently. Gareth Southgate's England football team have famously undergone a profound cultural shift, in which he has brought in people like Owen Eastwood and created an environment where there seems to be a greater sense of cohesion and enjoyment among the players. The team's performance under Southgate has improved dramatically – England reached the World Cup semi-final in 2018 and the final of Euro 2020 – but it was a comment during the World Cup in 2022 that caught my eye, in which England defender John Stones said, 'We spoke in our meeting about not letting any standards drop. Whether it might be putting out socks the right way for the kit men – we get on at each other for things like that because we have created those standards. Those little things matter and those little things keep you on the right path.'

In any environment, if the policing of the culture is coming from a manager it loses its impact over time. But coming from a colleague or a teammate? It hits home a lot more and creates an environment in which everyone is working towards the best possible standards, even in seemingly small ways. It instils discipline and respect. In an environment like the All Blacks, you should be grateful to be in it and look to make the most of it and look after it, never taking anything for granted.

The way in which we drove our culture was through the coaches empowering the players to police it, in the same way that they had the players deliver the game plan. The coaches would of course be in the background ensuring that everything was running smoothly, but the onus was on the players. With the likes of Tana Umaga and Richie McCaw heavily involved right from the start, working closely with the coaches, alongside a rigorous player-driven onboarding process, it built an environment whereby the coaches could be quite 'hands off' because they knew they had equipped the players sufficiently to drive it themselves.

WHO DRIVES YOUR CULTURE?

Think about how this idea might be applied in your own working environment. If your manager is the one constantly challenging you and your colleagues, it's a bit like the teacher disciplining the students or a parent constantly reprimanding their child. Coming from the same person higher up in the hierarchy all of the time inevitably means the message becomes muted. But if you have been empowered to enforce the standards in your organisation through having a clearly defined culture, a rapid onboarding process and recruitment based on character, then this policing can become peer-to-peer led. Instead of your manager, it's your colleague delivering the demand to pick up your standards. It's you delivering some difficult feedback to your peers. A leader's role might then become one more of moderator, ensuring that peer-to-peer feedback is being delivered in a manner that isn't personal and that nothing petty or egotistical is getting in the way. Working together, we're all striving towards excellence, and the policing of any cultural issue should remain focused on the issue and not the individual (play the ball, not the man). We'll talk more about delivering challenging feedback in Chapter 7 (Make Yourself Heard).

I think this attitude of self-sufficiency is instilled in us before we're even in the All Blacks environment. At Super Rugby level, where I played for the Crusaders, you arrive for training with all your kit in your bag, you train, put all your dirty clothes back in the bag and take them home and wash them yourself, before you get organised for the next day.

When I went to play in France for the first time in 2008, I couldn't believe it. It was all done for you! I would just turn up to training in my casual clothes, no need for a bag as my training kit would be waiting for me perfectly laundered and folded. I'd train, and then I'd throw all my kit in a bin and know it would be waiting for me all perfect again the next day. I'd then go upstairs, have a beautiful three-course meal waiting for me, eat and then put the plate away knowing the dishes would be sorted.

Now, don't get me wrong, it was incredible, but in New Zealand we'd think that was crazy: it's just not part of our culture. It's a little bit different with the All Blacks when you're in hotels, of course – it's not like you're expected to do your own washing – but at club level when you're going home each day you're expected to do it yourself as it teaches some really good habits. In France it was easy to see how you could relax a little bit, having everything done for you.

Is there a correlation between on-field performance and this kind of self-sufficiency? I'm not sure – and I hope I haven't spoiled it for any players by inspiring any team managers to go into their club tomorrow and say, 'Right, we're getting rid of the laundry service!' But what I do think it does is instil some discipline and sets standards to be maintained, which, when you're trying to grow an individual and a culture with ideas about gratitude and respect, certainly doesn't hurt. Though there are of course other ways to show gratitude and ensure

you don't get too comfortable, even if your laundry is done
for you.

HOW CAN I HELP THE TEAM?

In the later stages of my career, when I'd been living the All
Blacks values and been steeped in the culture for years, if I
wasn't selected in the team I would be able to see it from a dif-
ferent perspective from when I first broke through. I would
still be disappointed, of course, but by this stage I was in the
leadership group and we had a different environment: we were
now the backbone. I understood the importance of the team
far more than when I'd first come into the environment. I'd
find it hard at first when I was left out of the side, but then it
would give me more motivation to help the team.

But it's different when you're injured. When you're injured
your mind takes off – that's when you can really get absorbed in
yourself as an individual. If it's a serious injury, which we'll
talk about in more depth in Chapter 6 (Resilience), that's it –
you're out of the team environment. It's really important that
you do your rehab so that you can come back stronger *to help
the team.* I'd always have the feeling that I was letting the team
down by being injured, and that would offer some motivation
to get through my rehab, do it right.

But then you can also go into this little hole of *Me, me, me,*
and if your injury is minor – a little niggle or hamstring strain –
and you're still in the team environment, that can be dangerous.
It can threaten this idea that no one is greater than the team.

You might sit in a team meeting, not saying a word. You've clocked off for the time being. You're not playing the next match. The most challenging thing for anyone in this situation then becomes, *I can't play, so how do I contribute?*

I would look at the leadership group and team meetings, and ask myself, *Am I giving everything that I've got?* At my little mini-group meeting with the 9s and 10s, *Am I driving that to the best of my ability?* That was the hardest thing to learn for me: that I was still able to contribute despite not playing and being injured. Saying to myself, *Let's not let my ego get in the way here, I still need to help this team. I need to help them grow.*

While injuries aren't so much of a factor in the workplace, other setbacks can lead you to question whether you're still contributing as much as you would be normally. If you've been passed over for a promotion or you haven't been successful in getting the pay rise or bonus you were hoping for, that little hole of *Me, me, me* can be a tempting one to crawl into. But in the right environment, in which you're invested in enhancing the legacy of the jersey, the pathway back to doing what is best for the team should become clearer again soon.

In every team environment there are moments when decisions need to be made, and sometimes it becomes a choice between what is best for the team and what is best for the individual. If your personal purpose is aligned with the collective purpose of the organisation, in a strong culture where the values are lived every day and there is trust and a shared mindset between teammates and managers, those decisions become so much easier. But that's not to say there aren't sacrifices to be made or that people don't fall short of these standards from time to time (me included).

People make mistakes, and sometimes they make decisions that aren't for the best of the team – they might go out for a drink when they know they shouldn't, react badly to being left out or passed over for a project, or take credit for the work of others – but the important thing is that lessons are learned and sacrifices are made afterwards to show the coaches and your teammates that you are prepared to put the team first. Because ultimately, if you're not able to get over your ego and disappointment so that you can contribute to the team when you're left out of the side, if you're not able to demonstrate that you can put the team first, then there is no place for you in any high-performing organisation.

I've witnessed certain environments where at the start of every season it's, 'OK, so what are our values this year? Respect, honesty . . .' They're just words, and whether you live them or not, no one really cares. In this kind of environment it's no doubt easier to make decisions that aren't always for the best of the team. But when you have that marriage of collective and individual purpose, when you have leveraged your past to build a culture where *enhancing the legacy* is the name of the game, where you have star players living the very same values that are expected of new, young players, it makes it possible to look at every decision and instinctively know **what's best for the team**. After that, the decision takes care of itself.

THREE POINTS - HUMILITY

1. What's best for the team? The filter for any decision in any organisation.

2. Better people make better All Blacks: recruit on character and help your people grow.

3. Your people drive your culture: onboard newcomers rapidly into the environment and empower them to drive it themselves.

It was my first taste of the power of learning to manage your mind, and I was an instant convert. But it was also my first taste of something just as powerful: learning not only that it's OK to ask for help, but that it's absolutely vital.

CHAPTER 4

MIND MANAGEMENT

At the start of my career, people would think there was something wrong with you if you were getting help from the team psychologist. By the end of my career, they'd think there was something wrong with you if you *weren't*.

Towards the end of 2005 I was on a bit of a high, after a fantastic first three years of playing professionally. I'd just come off the hugely successful Lions series and a victorious Tri Nations series, and I'd had plenty of attention for my performances. It's fair to say I thought I was pretty good. Perhaps even in danger of getting a little ahead of myself.

We arrived in Wales for our end-of-year tour. We trained, and then a group of us went for drinks in the hotel. A few drinks turned into a few more, and next thing we knew it was well past the curfew. At six o'clock in the morning we thought it would be a good idea to jump in a taxi and head to another country: we asked the only driver we could find willing to take the fare to drive us to London.

It's a long drive, Wales to London, and suffice to say by the time we got to London we began to realise that perhaps, maybe, you know, after all, it wasn't such a good idea for a group of international rugby players to continue their night throughout the next day in another country when their teammates, coaches and entourage were all going about their day in Wales.

By the time we got back to Wales we knew we were in trouble. That Sunday night, a players' meeting was called. We were held accountable in front of our peers, which was a hugely important part of our player-driven culture. We were absolutely drilled by our captain, Tana Umaga, and rightly so. Tana carried a huge amount of mana in our team: he always had the players' backs and crucially he liked to have a good time – at the *right time*. Having Tana publicly point out how you've let the team, the culture and the black jersey down delivered a far more powerful wake-up call than the same admonishment from the coaches would have done. This isn't a telling-off from your teacher – it's coming from the classmate you hold in the highest regard, one of the people you're in this together with.

In the days that followed I couldn't think about anything else: *I've let down my family, I've let down my friends, I've let down my teammates, the fans, the black jersey.* My energy was sapped because I was ruminating over it, constantly thinking about my mistake. And then the story was out in the media, and it was the first time my name had been in the press for the wrong reasons. After all the positive attention I'd received for my performances on the field, it was a shock to me. And I couldn't handle it.

*Who do these guys think they are, behaving like they're big-
ger than the team? No respect for your teammates, the coaches
and management. No respect for the All Blacks who have gone
before. Leave the jersey in a better place? You're giving the
middle finger to the past.*

Given the opportunity, I can be quite prone to introspection.
Thinking things through too much, ruminating over the past,
castigating myself for my stupid mistakes – it's not difficult for
me to fall down into a hole with all this running through my
head, and it certainly wasn't hard at this stage in my career. All
I could focus on was the negative. I couldn't get in the right
state of mind to train to the level I knew I had to before a Test
match. I knew how badly I'd messed up, how what I'd done
contravened everything we'd tried to build in this culture.
**Better people make better All Blacks, no individual is bigger
than the team** – everything we'd done flew in the face of this.

Had I got carried away? Started to believe my own press?
How could we have been so stupid? Round and round it went.
I was digging a hole of my own making. I couldn't see any way
out. And for the first time in my career, I knocked on the door
of Gilbert Enoka, our mental skills coach, and asked for help.

LIVING IN THE NOW

From the beginning of my time in sport, we've always had the
psychologist, the mental skills coach – the 'head' coach, as we
often called them – in the fold. They were always in meetings.
Gilbert Enoka would work on the vision of the team. In 2003,

a World Cup year, he and the coaches would work out who we were and how we were going to win together. *What's going to help bring us together and be successful?*

I always knew they were an important part of the team, trying to give us our identity, but I never realised just how much I could use them on a personal level to work out my own identity. *Who I am. How I get the best out of myself.* All that changed when I knocked on Gilbert's door and said, 'I need help. I can't play this week – my mind is all over the place. I just can't focus on rugby – it's the least of my worries.'

Gilbert Enoka is a magician, a master of mind skills who has been in the All Blacks environment since 2000. But the first bit of advice he gave me when I went to see him was incredibly simple: *breathe.*

Often when you're in a state like I was then, your mind's racing and you're breathing heavily. I focused on my breathing and my heart rate went down, simple as that. Nothing revelatory there, but it's incredible what a difference having someone point it out to you can make. We forget the simplest things when our mind is rushing off elsewhere.

Then Gilbert proposed a process to get me focused on living in the here and now, rather than obsessing about all the things that were out of my control. We started by concentrating on what I was doing *right here, right now.* He made me write down every hour of the next twenty-four-hour period. 'We're only going to focus on the now slots in the next twenty-four hours,' he said.

So, I wrote it all down on a piece of paper. At six o'clock the next night, I wrote: '*Dinner at 7pm. Stretch session at 8.*

Attacking strategy meeting at 8.30. Swim recovery at 9. Bed by 10. Sleep till 7am. Wake up and breakfast at 7.30. Team meeting at 8. Training from 9 till 12. Lunch 12.30–1.30. After-noon training till 6pm.' All of a sudden, I had something to focus on other than the incident.

Then Gilbert said, 'Over the next twenty-four hours your mind is going to drift. It's going to keep wanting to go back to the incident. Your mind just wants to keep exploring your mis-take, and that's natural, but what I want you to do is, every time you catch yourself thinking about it, give yourself a slap on the leg and say, "What do I need to be thinking *RIGHT NOW?*" '

I carried around my piece of paper for the next twenty-four hours. I'd check it and see, 'Oh, I've got my pool recovery next, let's focus on that.' I would keep thinking about the past and the people I'd let down, as well as the future: *Oh, I can't play this weekend. I wonder what my parents are going to think. What is Honor going to think?* All the little things I couldn't control, my mind was drawn like a magnet to. Each time this happened, I kept bringing my mind back to the now: *I can't change the past or control how people react to things. These things are out of my control. But what I can control is these twenty-four hours.*

I would meet with Gilbert when the twenty-four hours were up and talk about how it had gone – what went well and what didn't, the times I found it harder to concentrate on the present. Then we'd do the same thing for the next twenty-four hours.

I found it a hugely powerful process, but I'm not saying it was easy. I found it really hard when I was trying to go to sleep at night. I'm usually a very good sleeper, but I really struggled with it during this period. My mind would be whirring and I'd find it very hard to stay in the present when trying to get off to sleep: it's not like it's an activity, like a swim, that you can throw yourself into and concentrate on in the present. You're just lying there, trying hard not to try too hard to do it . . .

Gilbert shared some breathing techniques with me to help at these more challenging times; there was one in particular where I would take three really deep breaths, into my belly not my chest, and in through my nose and out through my mouth to help relax and focus. Again, simple stuff, but I found it helped.

As the week went on and we reviewed each twenty-four hours, what I found was that I was thinking about the incident less and less. I was increasingly living in the present. I knew what I had to do next, so I did it. The negative thoughts were still there, of course, but I felt more able to manage them. Suddenly I felt ready to play again.

Come the weekend, I had one of the best games I've ever played in the black jersey, scoring the record amount of points by an All Black against Wales in history. It was my first taste of the power of learning to manage your mind, and I was an instant convert. But it was also my first taste of something just as powerful: learning not only that it's OK to ask for help, but that it's absolutely vital if you're serious about thriving in a high-performance environment. In fact, it's vital if you want to look after yourself and reach your true potential in any discipline.

SEE OPPORTUNITY, NOT FEAR

Turning to our mental skills coach for the first time in my three years as a professional was a pivotal moment for me. I knew he was there to help the team before that, but I hadn't understood the power of using him as an individual. I would come to use him more regularly after that, and after 2007 and our World Cup exit to France, seeing him and his team simply became part of the routine. It was the same for many of my teammates. What's important to stress here is that none of this was forced upon us. Gilbert and the mental skills coaches obviously played a role in the team as a whole, but on an individual level it was simply a resource that was there to use if we chose to. You can't force people to do this; they have to want to do it and they have to be ready. And, crucially, some people need it more than others.

If we were away on tour, such as a November series for four weeks, I knew I needed to see Gilbert every week. Every Sunday night, when I wrote my plan for the week ahead, one of the first things I'd put in would be 'cup of tea with Gilbert' on the Tuesday.

In 2015 we were preparing for a World Cup quarter-final match against France in Cardiff, a place where there was a lot of pain and hurt from our defeat there against them eight years before. *How am I going to deal with that?* I thought to myself. The last thing I wanted was to get to the game and have all these emotions come back to me, to think, *Oh no, I can't focus. I remember this changing room, with all the guys with their heads between their legs.* Or to have the French face up to us while we do the haka, as they so famously did in 2007, and think, *This is like history repeating itself . . .*

So, I'd talk with Gilbert about these thoughts and situations – about these *feelings* – and one thing we talked about very early on was that when the game finished in 2007, I'd sat outside and watched the French celebrate.

Gilbert said, 'So if we went back to that moment right now, what is the one thing you would want?'

'I'd want to play them again,' I replied.

'Where would you want to play them?'

'Right here.'

'In what context?'

'A World Cup play-off game.'

'Well, look,' Gilbert said. 'Eight years on you've got that exact opportunity. This is what you wanted.'

All of a sudden, I could see this situation for what it was: a real opportunity. *Man, this is exciting,* I thought. *This is unheard of. It feels like a message from above: getting to rewrite the wrongs of eight years ago.*

I was hugely excited – it was a challenge I desperately wanted and I walked towards it. We went out and put sixty-two points on France in a quarter-final – an incredibly special moment. But then I'd see him the following week, prior to our semi-final against South Africa. I'd injured myself while playing against France and couldn't train all week thanks to my bad knee. I thought for sure that my World Cup hoodoo was back.

'You keep thinking about the past,' Gilbert explained, 'about past World Cups where you've been injured. You keep self-pitying: "Oh, man, I'm injured again." But go back to the process, just write down the next twenty-four hours. You're not training because you're injured. You love doing your kicking session with the ball, but how about you do it with visualisation?'

Again, I'd map out my next twenty-four hours. I'd go out onto the training ground for my kicking session, where I'd normally do my twenty kicks, but this time I visualised it. I'd put my tee on the ground, visualise my run-up and the ball going through the posts, and then move on to the next one. It gave me confidence despite my not being able to physically do it, and it kept me focused on a process that was so vital to my success as a player.

I'm not saying all of this was easy, but by having these processes to return to, it really helped. In big tournaments I'd really rely on people like Gilbert.

ARE YOU REALLY PRESENT?

How is your 'now' focus? I've been fortunate to play with some outstanding leaders in sport and to meet some top business leaders, such as Bernard Arnault, at the time of writing the world's richest person, who in the 1980s had the ambition to create a luxury brand group and today is chairman and CEO of LVMH, the world's largest luxury goods company; his right-hand man Michael Burke, former chairman and CEO of Louis Vuitton, who has played a major role in making LVMH the global player it is today and, as Arnault puts it, 'has extended Louis Vuitton's lead over competitors and promoted the heritage of Louis Vuitton while anchoring it in modernity'; and Jim Ratcliffe, founder, chairman and CEO of INEOS Group, a chemicals company, who made a name for himself by buying unloved assets from other companies and turning them into much more profitable ventures, and who has sporting interests in his portfolio such as INEOS Grenadiers cycling team and French Ligue 1 football club OGC Nice.

All three of them are world-leading in their respective fields, but if I had to narrow down the one common trait that I noticed in all of them – and in all the great leaders I've played with – it would be their phenomenal 'now' focus. Each of them just gave off a sense that their minds work differently to the rest of ours, as they seemed to come up with creative concepts, seemingly on the spot, as we spoke – and yet they were incredibly present and engaged. They must meet hundreds of people a day and have so many things vying for their attention that it would be understandable for them to not appear to be in the moment, to be distracted by other things – and yet that wasn't the case at all. They were incredibly present – they had that ability to flick a switch and be incredibly now focused.

I've been able to bring this kind of mind management to games, of course, where it's critical to be present, totally focused on what you're doing *right now*. But it was a revelation to bring it into my everyday life. This kind of mind management, in which you're able to filter out distractions, organise all the things going on in your head and just focus on what you're doing *right now* is a key skill to deal with the challenges you face in any walk of life. But as with any skill, it can be improved upon with practice. Mindfulness apps, screen breaks and the kind of process-driven schedule that Gilbert used with me can all help us be more present and to manage our minds to the best of our abilities. And while we might not be functioning on Bernard Arnault's level (who is?), we can at least ensure we're improving on our own level each and every day.

YOUR MIND NEEDS HELP IN GOOD TIMES AS WELL AS BAD

The mental skills coach was an excellent place to turn when times were tough. But what I came to realise was, *Why do I need to wait for something to happen before I go see him? Why not use this resource more proactively?*

So, I'd go to see him after I'd had a really good game, when I was on top. Which might sound strange, but that was when I was at my most dangerous, when I might, without even realising it, fall into the trap of being a bit more complacent. I might subconsciously relax a little, knowing I had a strong performance under my belt. It wasn't lost on me that my indiscretion in Wales came at a time when I was receiving a lot of plaudits and things were going very well for me.

Gilbert and I began to look at my preparation. 'Is your preparation genuine?' was a key question, which asked if I was preparing fully or if my mind was drifting back to the previous game, reliving how well I'd played then. Was I just ticking boxes, Gilbert would ask, or did I actually want to be great?

I shared my personal purpose with Gilbert, of course, and a lot of the work we would do had this firmly in mind. He was one of the people I would share my goals with and who would hold me accountable for them throughout the year. Gilbert spent quite a bit of time with me at the start of each year or each campaign. He knew I was good at writing goals, having focus and direction for the year or campaign ahead, and he wanted to hold me accountable for them. It's one thing me writing them down and keeping them to myself, and then no one really knows at the end of the year or campaign whether I've achieved them or not except me. But I always felt that if I told someone, I had to deliver them, and then we'd have a review. He was a good person to do that with.

'You want to be an All Black great,' he'd say. 'Now you're going to challenge yourself by going from great to great – having another great game on the back of your last one. How are you going to go about that?'

Again, it came back to making sure my preparation was genuine, that I was living in the present and not taking anything for granted. At the pool stage of the 2011 World Cup I had a great game against France as part of a great team performance in which we beat them 37–17. This was the biggest game in the pool, against the best other team in it with whom we had history, not least in the 2007 World Cup quarter-final. Our next game was against Canada and, no disrespect intended towards Canada, but am I going to prepare as well as I did against France? Clearly not – you know subconsciously you don't have to prepare to the same standard.

But you still have to win. And allowing yourself to relax or cruise isn't what greatness is – certainly not in that All Blacks environment. You have to find ways to make sure your preparation is genuine. So, look at the week before, look at how you prepared against France. What was good about it? Take what was good from that and make sure you do more of it; improve on it where you can, so when you get into the lead-up to the Canada game you think, *I've set myself up even better than I did against France.* And if you've got the preparation and the thought process done, then you're all set up to play well in the game.

Then, of course, it all comes down to the game. If you don't perform well and don't deliver on the pitch, it's because something mentally hasn't had the same drive. But with Gilbert's help I was able to use the processes he first helped me with in Wales to help me focus on the now. I would have a few critical things to focus on – say, 'Attack the line, fast line speed, huge accuracy in my passing' – and know that if I did these three fundamentals well then I would have a good game. Just a simple reminder of what I had to do *in the now* would help me focus.

I had a few occasions in my career when I would have a great game and couldn't back it up. But if you want to be an All Black great you have to back it up – there's no point having a good game and then a poor one. An All Black great strings back-to-back performances together. I got much better at achieving that sort of consistency later in my career, so that it became a source of pride. It's probably one of the hardest things to do, to have success after success – to go from great to great again. You build yourself up for success and then it happens, and subconsciously you relax. You just think it's going to happen again, but it doesn't. You have to actually break it down to why you were successful, and strive, have a growth mindset to get even better before you can look at doing it again.

IS YOUR PREPARATION GENUINE?

Are you capable of following success with success – of going from great to great? It's easy to relax after success, but if your aim is high performance then you need to put steps in place to guarantee you can back your success up. Why go from acing a business-critical pitch to barely participating in a humdrum meeting? There can't be any shortcuts in your approach, no matter how easy you might feel the next challenge is: complacency is the enemy of success. Instead, make sure your preparation is genuine, don't take anything for granted, focus on your process and make yourself accountable – whether that's through writing goals down or, even better, holding yourself accountable to a colleague or leader. Because whether it's a business-critical pitch that promises glory or an unappealing meeting in the calendar, it's consistency that holds the key to true high performance.

REALLY, WE'RE GOING TO TALK ABOUT OUR FEELINGS?

At the start of my career my feelings towards dealing with the mental side of my preparation were markedly different to how I felt about it towards the end. *Really?* I'd think at the beginning of my career. *We're going to talk about our feelings?* And, as a humble Kiwi, *We're going to talk about walking the path to greatness? I'd rather stick to the small talk, thanks . . .*

Things are changing, of course, but I think for a lot of people in their jobs and lives it's a side of things they might shy away from, just as I did at the start of my career. It can be an intimidating process, to open up to a colleague and share what you're feeling, what you're striving towards, but it's an essential one if you're serious about reaching the peak of your potential.

As a young boy growing up in a country town in New Zealand, you just weren't supposed to talk about your feelings. Traditionally, with my generation and my parents', as a bloke you're just supposed to roll up your sleeves and get on with life. But as idyllic and beautiful as the tourist brochure for New Zealand is, we actually have a high suicide rate per capita, not to mention the highest adolescent suicide rate in the developed world,* and the suicide rate among males outstrips that among females by a significant margin.

It's not my place nor within the scope of this book to look at the reasons for this, but I do have the experience of being part

* https://www.unicef-irc.org/publications/pdf/RC14_eng.pdf

of a culture of stoicism among New Zealand men, bottling it up and keeping it inside, which I believe has some part to play in it. When I first walked into the All Blacks environment it wasn't exactly a place where people were talking about their feelings. But that has changed, to a large degree thanks to the younger players, the millennials coming through, and the development of wellbeing groups. The stigma around it is subsiding, and some crucial steps were taken during my time in the All Blacks.

Just being able to talk about problems or stresses or concerns – things going on inside your head – can make such a big difference on both a personal level and for the team – and can lead to growth. We had one session in our leadership group, in 2013, when we all got together for the first time following the Super Rugby season, and we were going around the group discussing how we were feeling. We did this regularly, and more often than not, even if I wasn't feeling good, I would say, 'All good – doing great.' I'd be done in a matter of seconds. But on this occasion I decided to open up and say how I was feeling about being back in the environment on a personal level. I'd had injury problems and I told my teammates that I felt I'd been struggling for motivation throughout the Super Rugby season, and I thought I'd lost my love for the game. Once the Crusaders had got through to the play-offs, I'd felt my motivation returning, but now that I was back in the All Blacks environment I could feel myself struggling again: the 2015 World Cup seemed so far away.

Through being vulnerable, I learned that I wasn't alone: a couple of the other guys in the leadership group were feeling the same. The other guys spoke about their own experiences and how they were feeling, and it felt like a huge amount of growth had taken place in this leadership group, that we had got to a position where we were able to be vulnerable in front of our peers, and you really felt you had the other players there to support you.

Gilbert Enoka saw this as a challenge and made sure systems were put in place for people who were feeling like me to reconfirm the importance of setting goals, driving standards and making sure the environment was a fun one, that we loved coming in to work each day. But he also knew some of us needed to be monitored regularly.

As soon as I started talking about how I was feeling, a huge weight lifted from my shoulders. It felt good to be sharing it with players who were in a similar frame of mind to me, and once the burden of bottling this up had been lifted, I then found it easier to put in the work to set some goals and get myself more motivated for the matches ahead. There was great power in knowing I wasn't alone.

The best leadership meetings, where we got the most growth, were when we were either being vulnerable and open, or we were challenging each other, which can make for quite a different atmosphere. It might be that people were challenged on what they were just saying, or whether what they were saying was what they truly believed. And once you get to what someone truly, strongly believes, and you're not just sitting there ticking boxes and saying what people want to hear, that's when you get growth.

Of course, meetings of this kind require a guiding hand. That's where someone like Gilbert would really come to the fore. He would guide us through these meetings, probing at times to get to the heart of what we were trying to talk about. Without someone facilitating things like he did, things can descend into chaos pretty quickly, especially when emotions are running high. If you just open it up, say, *Right, let's share what we're thinking, guys*, it can go all over the place. Each individual is dealing with so many different things that sharing actually becomes more of a hindrance, because you're pushing your anxiety or your pressures or your feelings onto other people who are also dealing with their own thing. But if you have structure, and a skilled moderator guiding you through the process, it can be incredibly valuable.

What also helps is having some diversity in your team. You want a good range of characters and personality types in your group to provide some balance. For someone like me, being able to be vulnerable and share things was of help to me, but it isn't necessarily for everyone. Some people genuinely don't need to do it. You don't necessarily want a group of people desperate to share, potentially to overshare, and that's why it was good to have characters like Tony Woodcock and Andrew Hore, who were more of the 'shut up and get on with it' types. That's true to who they are, it's not just a front they put on, and it provides some much-needed balance to those who feel they need to share in order to help not just themselves but the group.

BEING WELL

As I've said, I can be prone to introspection, rumination and mind churn. I've been in some pretty dark places during my career, as well as after my rugby career finished and the dreaded retirement was upon me. And I've found that talking about it, engaging in a process such as I did with Gilbert in my All Black days and have done with the likes of Kevin Roberts after I'd finished playing, has really helped give me some direction.

The mental skills provision through the likes of Gilbert felt like an extension of the **Better people make better All Blacks** ethos – it felt like the management really cared about us as individuals, not just as rugby players. I came to see it as an invaluable resource to help me improve as a player *and* as a person; it helped me through some difficult times and made me better able to handle the good times, too.

Throughout my time with the All Blacks I saw lots of sports science tools come and go: blood samples, testosterone checks, urine tests for hydration. Many of them would come in and out of fashion. But one thing that remained consistent pretty much throughout my time was a little wellbeing questionnaire we had to fill in every morning. It was just a very simple 'On a scale of 1 to 5 . . .' which asked how well we'd slept last night, how we were feeling. 'Any aches and pains?' It was a good way for the coaches and doctors to pick up on any potential injuries or problems before they happened. They might look and say, 'Dan's been tired the last couple of weeks – he could be susceptible to an injury. Let's get on top of that.' They would look at things like my sleeping behaviours, my nutrition, how much work I was doing outside the team environment. Or they might see that I have young children. Is it as simple as I need to stay in a hotel the night before each game? (And anyone who has young children will understand why I would always say yes to that one.)

If you're consistently scoring yourself low on how you're feeling, a significant number of ones or twos, then it might be a case that you need to have a conversation with someone, whether that's a coach or some specific mental or physical help. The long game, of course, is that this is better for the team – but it also made us feel valued and looked after as individuals.

This approach to wellbeing is pretty common now among the upper echelons of sport. Top teams realise how effective looking after their people is and it's considered an essential part of any high-performance environment. Businesses have cottoned on and some of the bigger companies have good wellbeing programmes, but I still feel they could learn a lot from sport when it comes to things like rest and recovery, at looking at the mental strain on their people. The impression I get is that it's viewed more as a 'nice to have' in business, rather than the essential it is in sport. If it isn't done right, though, it can become little more than a box-ticking exercise, which people can easily shy away from. *Really? We're going to talk about our feelings?*

But if it's done well, the potential for individual and collective growth is enormous. As a leader in any environment, checking in with your people regularly, monitoring their wellbeing, having an open door to any personal issues your people might be experiencing and just being aware of what they are going through goes such a long way to not only improving the wellbeing of your people, but also making your team perform more effectively.

At the end of my career, people were asking me: 'Hey, man, if you were just starting your professional career, what would you do differently?' And the simple answer is that I would use the mental skills people from day one. It took me three years to do it, but they really helped me – and I still probably didn't use it as much as I should have done. The improvements in my performance and life off the field have been significant, and crucially, it was the 'head' coaches who helped us learn to embrace the biggest mental hurdle to anyone trying to seek high achievement in life: performing under pressure.

THREE POINTS – MIND MANAGEMENT

1. In sport, we'd think there was something wrong with you if you weren't getting help from the mental skills coaches. Don't be afraid to ask for help – or to encourage your teammates to do so. I wish I'd done it sooner in my career.

2. Working on your mental skills and strength, both collectively and as an individual, is for the good times just as much as the bad: don't neglect them when things are going well.

3. Living in the now can help your worries about the past and your fear of the future: ask yourself, *What needs to be done now?* and focus on that task. And then the next one . . . If a team is doing this in unison, it can be a powerful thing.

There's never a game you won't go into the red; it's the ability to get out that counts. The less time you spend there, the more effectively you will be able to perform. That's winning.

CHAPTER 5

PRESSURE IS A PRIVILEGE

Pressure can do funny things to people. It can make a sure thing become a no-hoper when victory is in sight. It can transform effortless brilliance into rookie error, killer instinct into a soft touch. The greater the stage, of course, the higher the level of pressure. The margins between success and failure are so fine and yet can seem as wide as a chasm once the pressure really starts to bite. Failing to withstand the impact pressure can have on performance can earn a label no one ever wants: *choker*.

Being an All Black brings with it a very specific type of pressure. Learning about our whakapapa, the generations of those who have gone before and worn the black jersey, provides a vital sense of belonging, of what the responsibilities and expectations are and what our role in continuing them is. But that also brings pressure, to live up to the players and teams before us.

Then there is the expectation from our people. The New Zealand rugby team has an incredibly high win percentage in Test matches, but as high as that is, it's almost a redundant statistic when it comes to playing a Test match. We are expected to win *every* match, not almost 80 per cent of them, and to do so in style. Our supporters are fantastic, but there is no doubting what they expect from us. The All Blacks losing even a single Test match comes as a shock. The whole country can go into a minor state of depression if we don't win the World Cup.

We all have our eyes wide open to this before we even put on the black jersey. We all know what's expected in the All Blacks environment. Playing professional sport demands a certain capacity to tolerate pressure, as does high performance in any field. But we have learned to our cost that performing under pressure is something that can be learned and improved on, if you're willing to train your mind and push your boundaries.

In 2007 we lost a World Cup quarter-final to France in Cardiff. I might have mentioned that a few times already – and that's because it was such a pivotal moment for us. We went into that tournament as hot favourites, after an excellent couple of years under our new coaching trio of Graham Henry, Wayne Smith and Steve Hansen. We were gelling well and undergoing a cultural transformation. We thought we'd turn up and win, but instead we ended up becoming the worst-performing All Blacks side in World Cup history, outplayed and outfought by a strong French side.

It was a French side we'd beaten comprehensively twice already that year, but this team was a different beast entirely. They faced up to us and stared down our haka at the start of the game. We weren't expecting that. But we started the game

OK and were 13–0 up pretty quickly, despite not really click-
ing into gear. And then things started to go wrong.

By the time I went off injured in the second half the scores
were level. I already knew we were in trouble. We just weren't
prepared for the French onslaught. We hadn't really been in
that position before and we didn't know what to do. There was
a sense of incomprehension spreading throughout the side.
And when we were behind towards the end of the game, we
couldn't believe it. *How can we be losing? We hammered this
side by over forty points earlier in the year. This isn't supposed
to happen . . .*

From the bench, I looked around the team, and none of us had
the answers. There was a feeling that we didn't want to be there.
We weren't used to this. And we couldn't handle it. We were like
possums in the headlights – wide-eyed, in a state of shock, with
no idea what to do next. We weren't playing our game plan.

The French dumped us out of the competition. Not only
another World Cup opportunity gone, but now the worst-
performing All Blacks side in the history of World Cups. Just as
my sister was arriving in the country in anticipation of the semi-
final – *talk about getting ahead of ourselves* – I was on the plane
home with the team.

Fast-forward four years, and we're playing France again, in
the World Cup final this time. Again, we've comprehensively
beaten them recently – very recently, in fact, 37–17 in the
pool stage – but again, the knockout game, when the pressure
ratchets up several notches, is a very different situation. I'm
injured and watching from the sidelines as the boys hold an
8–7 lead and face a French onslaught. But this time it's

different. We're not possums in the headlights here. Yes, we're hanging in there at times, in survival mode, but this time the attitude is different.

We're clear. We're capable. *Yes!* The boys are saying, *This is what we've spent the last four years training for. We want this pressure. We need it. It means we're on the verge of greatness. We're walking towards it now, not running away from it.*

It was a complete change of mindset when we were under the pump, and we closed out the game by the slimmest margin in World Cup history to finally win a tournament we seemed to go into as favourites every time and yet come up short. It wasn't the soaring spectacle fans might have hoped for from a traditional All Blacks side, but it was a win ground out by a very new style of All Blacks team, able to play thrilling rugby *and* play ugly in a pressure-cooker environment.

What happened in those four years to take us from a team unable to handle pressure to one that walked towards it and welcomed it with open arms? And what can our experience teach you about how to handle pressure in your own lives?

RED HEAD/BLUE HEAD

Some people look at failure as all doom and gloom – and at the time it is. We'll talk in the next chapter about how necessary it is to make time to process those feelings. But failure also presents opportunity: to accept what went wrong and learn from it. And what can come out of that failure is greatness. That's how you need to look at it. Spend time learning, reviewing, ask questions, challenge each other – then repurpose and look at what's going to drive us forward.

After our failure at the World Cup in 2007 we broke down why we'd been unsuccessful, and it was clear that our inability to handle the pressure was a big part of it. We just weren't prepared for what happened in that game. We were doing plenty of work on our physical preparation but not enough on the mental side. And after that, plans were drawn up to devote some significant time to our mental strength and learning the power of controlling our minds. It's my firm belief that the work on our mental game that started after the Rugby World Cup in 2007 provided the foundation for the All Blacks' strength and was a major reason why we were the number one team for almost a decade.

I talked about our mental skills coach Gilbert Enoka at length in the previous chapter, and he played an instrumental role in this process. One of the people he brought in was a forensic psychiatrist called Ceri Evans, who introduced the red head/blue head concept into the All Blacks environment.

Put simply, 'blue head' is when you're calm and clear, and your thinking process is focused on the here and now. It's the state you want to be in for as much as possible during a match or any pressure environment, as it's one where you're best able to make the right decisions and execute your skills effectively. 'Red head', however, is when you're no longer living in the now: you're thinking about something that's just happened or something in the future that you can't control. You're no longer in control of your mind.

In a game, particularly as a young player, I might make a mistake (in fact I would make some sort of mistake in every single game: no one is perfect). I might make a bad pass to a teammate who was running in for an almost certain try. Or concede possession from it. I would then run around for the next five minutes in a state of red, thinking, *I can't believe I made that mistake, such a simple skill! I have to make it up.* All of a sudden, I'm thinking about the outcome of that bad pass instead of what's immediately in front of me. I can't take that pass back – I can't stop what's just happened – but what I can focus on is my next task, though to do that I'm going to need to get back to a state of blue head.

There are three things your mind can do when it's in a state of red: *freeze, fight* or *flight.* I played with Ma'a Nonu a lot, and his primary red-head characteristic was fight. He would argue with the ref, scream at teammates and himself, maybe want to put in a shoulder charge to make up for it. In that state, his mind wasn't in control. It wasn't only Ma'a, of course – the majority of my teammates would go into 'fight' when in a state of red.

Other guys would go to flight – they just want to get out of there. *Oh, my hamstring's a bit tight. I keep making mistakes. I don't want to have to deal with this. What about the media if we lose? We can't lose.* Basically finding any excuse so they don't have to be the ones out there performing under pressure.

The final one is freeze – which was my primary characteristic. When I froze I would go quiet, and the last thing you want on the rugby field is a quiet number 10. My job was to direct the backs and our attacking play, but in a state of red my communication would be poor and my body language down. I'd be a possum in the headlights.

When Ceri Evans and Gilbert Enoka introduced this idea to us it just made total sense. It resonated with all of us. What was important to bear in mind was the fact that you're never going to go through a whole game without getting into a state of red. It's completely normal. But the key is to recognise when you're in this state and be able to bring yourself back to a state of blue where your thinking process is calm, where you're thinking about the here and now.

If you're running around in a state of red for five minutes before you get over it, it's detrimental to your team. Your mind is not in control, you're making poor decisions. Whereas if you have the tools in place to get back to a state of blue in only one minute, you're saving four minutes of the game where you can make a more positive contribution and make clearer, calmer, more productive decisions. We put a lot of emphasis on this, on bringing ourselves back to the here and now. The ability to understand when you're in the red is the key, so you can use your tools to get out of it.

There's never a game you won't go into the red; it's the ability to get out that counts. The less time you spend there, the more effectively you will be able to perform. That's winning.

WHAT IS YOUR RED-HEAD CHARACTERISTIC? FREEZE, FIGHT OR FLIGHT?

When the pressure ratchets up, are you like a possum in the headlights? Do you find yourself becoming confrontational? Or do you just want to get the hell out of there? Start to recognise how you react to pressure situations. Once you're looking for it, you'll be better able to know when you're in the red.

Of course, we're all capable of each one of these characteristics when we go into the red: we will all have times when we've been in fight mode, in the red, when we might lose our temper or argue with someone, even against our better judgement. Just as we're all capable of flight or freeze. But it's the primary one we go to in pressure situations that is the key to identify and become used to recognising. The first step is to know when you're in the red, before you can do anything about getting out of it.

FOCUS ON THE PROCESS

During any task, it's so easy for your mind to start to drift towards the future, towards outcomes and results. Your mind might wander towards all sorts of things that will distract you from the process that needs to be completed. In a pressure situation this becomes exaggerated. During a game, my mind could start to ask, *What if we lose? What if I miss?*

Being the kicker in a rugby team brings with it a unique kind of pressure. When I'm lining up a kick, I'm not executing a skill instantly as I would when the game is flowing. I'm more like a football penalty-taker who has plenty of time to think before he or she takes the kick. And as too many penalty-takers to mention can relate, often that time to think is the last thing you need.

It's easy as a kicker for me to get to the back of my run-up and think, *I need this to win the game.* Or how about, *I missed my last two kicks – I can't mess this one up.* Or maybe even, *I'm going to let so many people down if I don't get this right . . .*

None of these thoughts are going to help. They're only going to add to the weight on your shoulders, increase the burden of anxiety. They're going to put you in a state of red, and you need to find ways to stop your mind drifting. You need a process to focus on and help you deal with the pressure in that moment.

I see it a lot with kids – they are so fixated on the outcome, on wanting to win. As parents we can be guilty of putting too much pressure on young people, filling their heads with outcome-based thoughts. And yes, the outcome is important – building that competitive edge – but so is having fun, on losing yourself in the process and improving. By focusing on the right process, the outcome will take care of itself. And if it doesn't then you review and you iterate, until you get that process right.

When I teach kicking to young players, I tell them to develop a routine that is the same for every kick you take. That's your process, and you need it to be consistent if you want to deliver a consistent outcome. This was my process:

I grab the ball and find the valve. More often than not the valve is along the seam. I put the ball on the tee with the seam in line with the posts. I take five steps back and double-check the ball is lined up correctly. I then find a little space between the posts – it could be something in the crowd, or a cloud or billboard – to aim for. I tell myself to breathe. Now I go three steps to my right, and this is when your mind can really start playing games with you. What if I miss? What will 50,000 people think? All the people at home? I take another breath, tell myself to relax, focus on the ball, look up, find that spot again between the posts. I look down, look up, visualise the ball flying between the posts (visualisation is a really important part of my kicking process). I look back down at the part of the ball I'm aiming to kick (the sweet spot); I tell myself to breathe, breathe again, then I go into my run-up and kick the ball.

Because I have these key parts of the process, I can focus on doing them to help my mind stop thinking about the outcomes. If I follow every part of this process every time then I know I'll have consistency, and the more consistency in the routine and process there is, the more consistency you have in the result. As Gilbert Enoka says, 'When the pressure is at its highest, champions don't necessarily raise their game – they just deliver brilliant basics.'

I've chosen kicking to illustrate one of my key processes, but you can break just about anything you do down to its core process. In your own working environment, you must first ensure that your process is the optimal one – something that can only be achieved through trial and error, and iterating each time. It's so important to be open to evolving your process, with the ambition being to create one that you can then deliver consistently, so that when the pressure's on, it's a familiar, well-worked and effective one that you can reliably fall back on to deliver consistent results. For the things you have to do regularly as a leader when the pressure's on – whether that's presenting, writing reports, moderating meetings, breaking bad news or coaching challenging members of your team – there will be a process you use. If this is a consistent one that you know you can trust, you're going to be better equipped to deal with delivering it in a pressure-cooker environment – though that's not to say it will be easy, of course.

––––––––––

AND IF IT'S HARD TO FOCUS ON THE PROCESS...

Much like the 'next twenty-four hours' that Gilbert Enoka asked me to focus on in the previous chapter, my process keeps my mind anchored in the present. In the now. But it's certainly not an infallible process. It's not perfect every time. There will be times when, at the back of my run-up, unhelpful thoughts will enter my mind. My mind will want to focus on the outcome, the final score or something else out of my control in that moment. It becomes a battle in my head: I'm fighting to get back to my routine, to stop thinking about the result.

In these moments I've found that I need to do something external, just to take me out of this mind fight. So, I'll push my toes into the ground, really concentrate on that, literally grounding myself. And just a couple of seconds of doing this takes me out of my mind, allows me to think about something else for a second. Then I go back to my routine: *OK, breathe, look up, visualise the ball going through the posts, look down at the sweet spot, tell yourself to breathe, move into run-up* . . .

When I caught myself in a state of red during a game – after I'd made a mistake or found my mind drifting – I would similarly do something external to get myself back in the game. If you've ever seen highlights of me playing and noticed I've just given myself a slap on the leg, you've witnessed me trying to get out of a state of red and into a blue-head mindset. A short, sharp shock and then, *Right, next job*. I'm accepting I've made a mistake and telling myself to focus on the next task.

I might be in a huddle and then look up at the scoreboard, see that we're down by eight points with only five minutes to go. *Oh no, what if we lose?* Slap myself on the leg. *Right, next job*.

You can take this approach into any pressure situation. I'm not for a second suggesting everyone should be going around whacking their leg every time they sense themselves slipping into a state of red, but you can find your own physical process to bring you back to the blue. In our team environment everyone had their own way of dealing with it. Breathing was a popular one, which is really helpful to take an individual out of a state of red. It can be something incredibly simple, but the intention is always the same: to bring you back to focus on the process at hand. *What's next? What's now?*

MANAGING PRESSURE COLLECTIVELY

I'd learned from a pretty young age the importance of a consistent process for a kicker, so in some ways I was already applying some of the techniques for dealing with pressure that we were bringing into the environment. But in open play I hadn't really developed anything like this, so it was a real revelation.

Perhaps the most useful aspect in the team environment was in learning our teammates' traits. What happened when they went into a state of red: freeze, fight or flight? When we learned this, we were able to spot the warning signs and help them out of it, to return to a state of blue. For Ma'a Nonu, I know he's in the red when I can see him getting aggressive, trying to physically right his wrong. When this happens, I need to give him a simple task, ask a clear question so that he has to think instead of running around on emotion. 'Hey, Ma'a,' I might say. 'Who's tackling you? What are you seeing?'

And it worked the other way round, of course. Ma'a might notice I've gone quiet, know that I'm in the red. 'Talk to me, Dan,' he'd say. 'You've gone quiet on me.' He knows that when I've gone quiet I'm no longer in control of my mind.

By applying these mental skills to look beyond your own performance and learn how your teammates handle pressure, you have another way to reduce the time anyone is spending in the red. Ma'a might catch me quickly, within a minute, and talk me round to a state of blue, so that's precious time I'm not spending in a state of red making poor-quality decisions and actions. That's extra time that I'm going to be a more effective player.

This examination of our holistic approach to handling pressure extended to looking at something which has always been seen as something of an advantage for us: the haka.

You're full of adrenaline when you go into a Test match. We'd perform the haka, this hugely significant cultural ritual that means so much to us, and we'd get very emotional, very worked up through this performance in which we bring up our spirit ancestors from the ground. *We're about to go to war.*

We asked ourselves, *Why are we giving so many penalties away in the first twenty minutes of the game?* And we put it down to the haka. We hadn't yet moved fully to a process-focused approach to the game, we were full of emotion and all collectively in a state of red. That's no way to start a Test match.

To tackle this, we changed our process. The team would now perform the haka, walk back to the 22-yard line, have a huddle and our captain would just tell us to breathe. Three really deep breaths to get our heart rates down, clear our minds, and then he would hand it over to the playmakers to tell us to focus on the first task and what that task is. If we're kicking off, it might be to ask a specific player to get up and compete for the ball. If we're receiving, it might be as simple as just saying, 'Catch the ball.' It's just a very straightforward process-based instruction to get us all aligned and focused on the task in hand.

It means you then have fifteen players lining up in a state of blue: it gives you better control and it completely changed our start to Test matches, cutting down significantly on needless mistakes and penalties.

CAN YOU SPOT WHEN YOUR TEAMMATES ARE IN THE RED?

It's one thing to be able to spot your own descent into the red, but we aren't thinking clearly when we're in this state and sometimes we need some outside help. I loved knowing what state my teammates would go into when they were in a state of red, so I could help them get back into the blue. This is going to require getting to know your teammates and recognising whether they go quiet when the pressure's on, or if they seem to become a possum in the headlights or even get quite worked up and argumentative. Equally, your teammates will learn to recognise your primary red-head characteristic. Recognising this early and helping a colleague or teammate out of the red and into the blue will ensure not only the individual but your team is more effective. You're going to need a people-driven environment where it is possible to be honest and vulnerable with colleagues to make this happen, of course, but if you're able to do the mind management work both individually and as a team, the collective results will be a major performance enhancer.

PRACTISING FOR PRESSURE

Learning to handle these moments of pressure isn't like a tap. You can't just turn it on when you walk onto the pitch. You need to be able to prepare and practise them, but that's quite a difficult thing to prepare for. After all, how do you recreate the pressure and intensity of a Test match environment on the training field? How can you prepare for that pressure moment at work when you're sitting quietly at your desk?

Our coaches would engineer things to not only reproduce that intensity, but to create scenarios more difficult than anything we'd encounter on the Saturday. I would do a lot of goal-kicking sessions with Wayne Smith. He would do everything he could to get me into the red state, running through various scenarios to take me out of my state of blue. He would randomise where I took my kicks from, challenge me with things like, 'You've missed your last three kicks from this spot,' and heckle me throughout my routine to try to provoke a response. The more you practise, the easier it is in the game.

Our training on a Thursday before the Test match would often be tougher than the game itself. Sometimes the coaches might get a referee in and tell him to cheat: to sin-bin Richie McCaw for no reason so we're a man down for ten minutes, or to call fouls that never were. The coaches would want to see how we reacted to these scenarios, and often we didn't react well. But it's better to learn that in training than in the game.

This was high-intensity training but you'd only go full-contact for maybe twenty minutes – say four blocks of five minutes in which you had to give 100 per cent effort. You'd go from one play, and then have to sprint to the other end of the field for a lineout. The coaches would be hurrying us, putting us in difficult positions mentally and physically. You'd be playing with two balls, having to run for a breakdown at the other end of the field, all the time dealing with things happening quickly to see how you'd deal with it in the game. It was so challenging that, when it came to the game, you actually had a bit more time than you had in training. For starters, you're not playing with two balls.

To try to find that mental edge every week is one of the hardest things in sport, and we were fortunate to have mental coaches like Gilbert Enoka and Ceri Evans to do it. They'd even do things like try to engineer a poor training on the Thursday to add a bit of an edge to our preparation. If training's perfect all week and then you get smacked in the first twenty minutes of the game then it's going to come as a surprise: you're not going to expect that after training so well. But if you have a bad Thursday session then you know it's time to switch on. *We should win this week,* you might think, *but we can't afford to get complacent.*

We also had the opportunity to dig deeper into our own individual limits and triggers to help us better maintain that state of blue in a match. Ceri Evans would run one-to-one sessions in which he would test us – probe and push us to try to get us out of our state of blue. He would ask really challenging questions, perhaps something about your upbringing or family. I don't know how he did it – I guess that's why he's such a specialist – but he was very good at getting me out of a state of blue and into my red head.

This was psychology on a whole other level. It wasn't for everyone – it was very confrontational and challenging. I'd walk away from an hour-long session with him absolutely exhausted, my brain completely unused to being worked in such a way. But there was also a real opportunity for growth, as I became better at being able to control my mind – to stay in a state of blue or to return to it quicker – and also about learning about myself as a person, digging really deeply into who I am as a human being.

He would confront you with all sorts of things you didn't really want to talk about: your upbringing, the difficulties you had as a child, the family situation that has shaped you into the person you are today. The death of my grandparents really affected me when I was young. I used to spend a lot of time with them when I was a child because my parents were often working. My dad's parents lived on the same street as us, and I used to spend a lot of time playing there with my cousins. I was about fifteen when Dad's dad died, and then both my mum's parents died a couple of years later. I was young and I didn't really know how to deal with my emotions then. As a down-to-earth country kid, I knew you weren't supposed to show your emotions like that. But I would open up in these sessions with Ceri, often feeling very drained but also feeling much lighter – like I'd got some weight off my shoulders and was more able to walk towards the challenge of my personal purpose.

I worked with Ceri a lot leading into World Cups, looking at why we'd been unsuccessful in the past. Richie used him a lot too. As I said, it wasn't for everyone. It was always an option, never forced upon us. But I could see real value in being better able to control my mind and knew I needed to get on top of it.

DO YOU PLAN FOR YOUR WHAT-IFS?

One of the biggest challenges in preparing to perform under pressure is posed by the uncertainties you'll face when you do it for real. It's really hard to plan for uncertainties, yet whether you're an individual, a business or a sports team, you can be sure some challenges you haven't prepared for will spring up.

In the rugby environment, you might have poor refereeing decisions that can change a game, a serious injury to a key player or you come up against opposition who do things you haven't prepared for. Just as in business there are countless uncertainties to be faced, especially when doing things like launching a new product or just starting out – the economy, large-scale competition, industrial disruption or even a global pandemic. So how do you deal with this?

In the All Blacks we'd have what-if sessions, in which we'd be challenged with scenarios like: **What if** . . . our captain gets a red card after twenty-five minutes and we have to play the rest of the Test match with fourteen men? **What if** . . . we're three points down with two minutes to play, do we take the shot to level it or go for the try and potential victory?

Within the group we'd have these conversations and develop plans for these moments. You hope these things don't happen, of course, but experience soon teaches you that something unexpected will. We used to be shocked by these, but following the work that we put into our mental preparation after 2007, we were able to deal with them so much faster. And even if we hadn't prepared for the specific uncertainty we encountered on the field, all the work we were putting into just dealing with uncertainty in general meant that we were less likely to be shocked by it and more able to respond quickly and effectively. We had the necessary cognitive practice of responding to the unexpected through our what-if sessions.

This is something American swimmer Michael Phelps famously put into practice during the 200m butterfly final at the Beijing Olympic Games in 2008. When his goggles filled with water during the race and he found himself swimming blind, he didn't panic. He'd trained in the dark before and crucially he had visualised overcoming problems like this before. He'd prepared for this during his what-if sessions. So, with goggles filled with water and unable to see, he counted his strokes instead of relying on his sight and duly won the gold medal in world-record time. When asked after the race what swimming blind had been like, he simply replied, 'It felt like I imagined it would.'

The challenge when thinking about your what-ifs is to introduce them into your own preparation for pressure situations. Whether you're preparing for an important presentation or about to launch a new venture, ask yourself, *What if . . . the worst that could happen did happen?* Work with your colleagues and your team on what your response would be, while remembering that it's always better to prepare for something far harder than what you eventually do encounter. That way, doing it for real will almost seem easier because you've done the work.

EMBRACING PRESSURE

Learning to improve our performance so significantly under pressure allowed us to become the dominant team in rugby and win back-to-back World Cups over the next few years. It was a complete mindset shift, to go from fearing that unfamiliar sensation on the field in Cardiff to learning to embrace pressure, to welcome it.

Because what we came to realise during this time is that **pressure is a privilege.** If you want to win World Cups and be the number one side, then you need to embrace those pressure moments. They are what comes with the territory, and if you're serious about high performance then you need to open your arms to them and thrive in these moments. You have to want to live in those moments. They should come to excite you, because only with that level of pressure can you grow and achieve things you haven't before.

After retiring from rugby, I knew that there were two things I would miss about the game above all others. The first is the camaraderie among teammates, that sense of belonging, the banter and the relentless challenging, pushing each other to new heights, which I talked about earlier in this book. And the second is that feeling of pressure, the butterflies, that buzz from trying to challenge myself, take me out of my comfort zone. I need that in my life – every single day, preferably. And I know that anyone I've ever met who has achieved great things – my All Blacks teammates, my coaches and the leaders in business – all have this trait in common. Anyone striving to do better needs it too.

I know that this next stage of my life needs to fill me with this feeling. It needs to offer me the opportunity to walk towards pressure. It's why I've done things like a twenty-four-hour kickathon for UNICEF, raising over half a million dollars towards providing clean water for kids in the Pacific. I did 1,598 kicks in the time, for which I had to train and prepare fully for months leading up to the event to make sure my body didn't break down. It was televised, which provided its own level of pressure, and I was heavily involved in all aspects of the production. It was a pressure I welcomed, though. A pressure I needed.

The thing I've come to realise is that the pressure I put myself under is far greater than any external pressure. Be it from tens of thousands of fans in a stadium, a tense Test match situation when we're behind in the dying moments, or being challenged by the opposition, nothing competes with it. I feed off it, and thanks to the work I've done on my mental skills it's a positive force for me.

If I don't get nervous or have to prepare for something – if I'm not getting the butterflies again – I feel like I'm just cruising through life. I want to challenge myself, to do new things. And this attitude, to look to try new things and embrace the pressure, is the difference between those comfortable to cruise, and those who want to aspire to their own level of greatness.

At the top level of sport, physical fitness is obviously important. The All Blacks pride ourselves on being the fittest team in the world, and late in a game, when you're really feeling it, it can be easier to slide into a red-head mindset if your fitness isn't quite there. Our strength and conditioning coach Nic Gill made sure we were in tip-top condition, never overworking us but ensuring all of our work was geared towards peak performance so that we were better able to control our minds in those latter stages of the match.

But all the best teams are in top physical shape. You might be able to get a slight physical edge – obviously you'd have to do the work – but at the very top the team's mental capabilities can be the difference between winning and losing. Some people who haven't done the same level of mental preparation as us might go into the red and want to be anywhere but on that field. But if you've done the work, you can embrace those moments, knowing that **pressure is a privilege** and you're on the verge of achieving excellence. You need to prepare for them so thoroughly that when they come around, you can just perform in the moment. You've done the work, now just play.

All the most successful people in the world live with pressure every day. If you have that kind of high-performance pressure in your life it means you're one of the lucky ones. Outside of rugby I now have to go out and find those opportunities, because I know it's such a privilege to have that kind of positive pressure in your life. If you can reframe pressure in your own life and work and come to see it as a privilege too, an *opportunity* that comes with the territory when you're pushing yourself and trying to get that little bit better each day, then you will soon learn to live for those moments.

THREE POINTS - PRESSURE IS A PRIVILEGE

1. Pressure can be your friend, if you're willing to walk towards it. You might come to find you live for those high-pressure moments.

2. What's your red-head characteristic: freeze, flight or fight? Learn your triggers. Find ways to get you back to blue faster.

3. Train at a level above the actual event, so when it comes time to do it for real it almost seems easier.

It's only by having the courage to challenge our own capabilities, to reach beyond where we *know* we can go, that we can hope to do great things – but at the same time risk failure.

CHAPTER 6

RESILIENCE

MANAGING SETBACKS

I n 2011 I was playing in my third World Cup. After our agonising defeat against France in the quarter-final of the 2007 competition, we were looking forward to making amends on home territory, attempting to break our twenty-year wait for a World Cup triumph. I was twenty-nine years old and in my prime. I'd trained hard, was injury-free and I felt great. *This is our time. This is my moment. We're going to break the All Blacks World Cup hoodoo. I've got a good feeling about this . . .*

By this stage in my career I was vice-captain of the team, but I'd never actually captained the side. Richie McCaw was our captain, of course, and it always seemed to turn out that whenever he didn't play, I didn't play either. All that was about to change, however.

We played France in the pool stages, and I had one of the best games I've ever played in the black jersey. I felt in complete control and my attacking game was exactly where I wanted it to be at that stage of the World Cup, as we ran out 37–17 winners. And then, before our last game in the pool stage, against Canada, Richie pulled out of the match because of his broken foot. It was a serious injury but, Richie being Richie, it wouldn't stop him playing in the rest of the tournament. I was named captain on the eve of this game.

It was a huge moment for me and my family. I got straight on the phone to my dad: 'I've just been made captain – I'm going to go in and do the press conference as captain!' I did the press conference and talked at length about reaching this huge milestone of captaining the All Blacks at last, about what a historical moment it was for me and my family, what an honour and a privilege it was. I then went off to training at Rugby League Park in Wellington.

The captain's run is a tradition in rugby, a light training session the day before the match led by the captain rather than the coaches. We'd always play a game of touch rugby to start it off, forwards against backs, just a bit of fun. During this light game, however, I rolled my ankle a little. Nothing too serious, certainly nothing to worry about, so I kept playing. Then we jogged through a couple of our plays and the game plan, which we do every captain's run, before the forwards would go off to practise their lineouts and some scrums, and the backs would kick the ball around.

This is when I would do my kicking routine. Normally I would take a set number, fifteen or twenty kicks at goal depending on the circumstances, but this time I decided to do a truncated routine of four. On my last shot at goal – and I've kicked millions during my career – I kicked the ball and then, *Argh!* The ball rolled a couple of yards in front of me and I fell to the ground in sudden, excruciating pain. I was screaming in agony, the pain in my groin was unbearable. It was a nightmare. *How can this be happening?*

Some people initially thought I might have been playing a joke, but I would never have done that. Graham Henry would get quite anxious just before Test matches so the last thing he'd appreciate is a joke like that. Wayne Smith was behind the posts catching the balls and he knew straight away it was serious. He came running to see if I was OK.

The pain was unbearable and yet actions for the good of the team were already being implemented: with the support of the doctor, I was rushed to the changing room as the media were on their way and we didn't want them to see me lying around injured the day before the game. There was a lot of redness, some internal bleeding around the site of the injury. At this stage I knew I was out of the game but I still held out hope: *Maybe it's just a partial tear and with some injections and some sort of miracle I'll be back in a couple of weeks . . .*

By the time I was on my way to the local medical centre for scans with Deb Robinson, the team doctor, I knew it was serious. When the results were ready I didn't want to look at them – couldn't bear to see them. Deb and the specialist discussed the injury away from me, at my request. I just wanted to get back to the hotel as soon as possible.

In the back of the car on the way to the hotel I couldn't take it anymore. I had to know. 'Deb, is my World Cup over?'

She said, 'Yes,' and then I just burst into tears. I felt

suddenly consumed by it all and I had no answer. Nothing. It was a moment when nothing made sense at all, and the disappointment poured out of me.

NOT EVERYTHING HAPPENS FOR A REASON

When we look at any high-performing figure, we only get a partial view of the picture. We see the success and the glory, but we very rarely bear witness to the hard work it's taken them to get there. The hours spent honing their craft, the dedication and mindset that has allowed them to rise above their competition. And while we might see some of the setbacks – reading in the papers that I'm injured and out of the World Cup, for example – we don't get to see just what it takes to come back from something like that.

I wouldn't be the man I am today if it wasn't for the setbacks, the difficulties and the injuries along the way. I've suffered huge setbacks as part of a team, such as our disappointment at the 2007 World Cup, and those of a more individual nature, the greatest of which, without exception, was this moment in 2011.

We live in a world that isn't perfect. Life isn't supposed to be – it throws you bad passes all the time. People don't always see that things aren't destined to run smoothly, and when they do have a setback along the way they can go into some pretty dark places. I should know – I've been there.

I fell deeply into a state of self-pity once I received the news that my World Cup was over. *Why me? Why so serious an injury? Why does this have to happen now, during the biggest moment of my career?* I couldn't answer these questions. Nothing made sense to me. I returned to my hotel room after the results and was not a pleasant person to be around. Honor came to see me but we didn't talk. We simply lay in silence, my mood smothering the room. Some of the players and coaches came in to visit. At the time, I didn't really want to see them. I wanted to be alone with my pain. Only later would I appreciate the fact that they'd come.

With any setback, there's a period when you try to rationalise it, try to make sense of it as if it's part of some bigger picture. I'd been able to do this with the first serious injury of my career, some two years before when I'd been playing for Perpignan in France during my first sabbatical from the All Blacks. In only my fifth game for the French side, I ruptured my Achilles tendon which meant I was out of the game for six months and didn't play again for Perpignan.

I immediately felt that I'd let everyone down. I'd let the club down, the fans, the players and the people who had paid me to go and play there. And then on a more personal level, I began to worry about myself. *Would I be able to return as the player I was before? Would I ever reach the heights again?*

I had a serious operation, my head filled with worry about the possibility that I wouldn't regain my pace afterwards. I had the All Blacks physio Pete Gallagher fly over to spend a couple of weeks with me when I started to learn how to walk properly again. It's really important to have the right gait, so when you start running again everything's how it's supposed to be. I came back within five and a half months, which was very fast, but it was more like eight months before I was back to being 100 per cent.

I was able to rationalise that setback. I was a firm believer that everything happens for a reason, and that injury was my body telling me I was playing too much rugby. I'd been through a full Super Rugby season in New Zealand, played in all the internationals that season, including the end-of-year northern hemisphere series, which was a successful Grand Slam tour for the All Blacks, then went straight to play in France when my body should have been resting. I came to accept that it was an injury caused by overload, which was of some comfort as I began the long, slow road back to recovery through rehab.

But in 2011, I had no such comfort. I was in good form, peaking at the right time. It was a freak injury, the timing unbelievably bad luck. I had nothing but my grief. And as I would discover, at the heart of that lay the route back from the greatest personal setback of my career.

TIME TO GRIEVE

The one thing I learned above all else during this period was that in order to overcome a setback, you must first make time to grieve. After the hospital I could have just said, *Oh, that sucks, but I'm going to bounce back and help the team.* Now, that's a nice idea, but trying to put that into practice in reality is a little more challenging. When you've suffered a major disappointment and a huge setback – when the dream you've been working towards your whole career is snatched away from you – even the greatest of team players is going to struggle to avoid the personal disappointment, the anger, the sadness – the *why me?*

And that's OK. In that period immediately after the injury I was in a dark place: I was incredibly down and depressed, and I couldn't stop ruminating. My mind was spiralling out of control, trapped in a vicious cycle, but during this period it's an important part of the process to go through. To let it all out – the anger, the frustration, the sadness and disappointment.

During this period, don't fight your feelings: if you feel like crying, then just let it out and cry. If you feel angry, then let go and allow yourself to be furious (safely, of course). This is the time to lie on your bed and stare at the ceiling, to rage at the injustice of it all. Think of it as the very opposite of focusing on the process to take your mind from unhelpful thoughts that we discussed in the previous chapter: it's time to indulge in the unhelpful thoughts.

But in a team setting, staying with intense feelings for too long can have a detrimental impact on the people around you. In sport, and in business, that's obviously not good for the team's long-term outlook. So, if you want the best for those around you – and for yourself in the long run – you need things in place to draw you back from your dark place.

Allowing yourself time to deal with your difficult feelings after a setback means you're building towards coming to terms with it. And acceptance is a necessary tool to develop to overcome setbacks. We have to learn to accept that setbacks are part of life, part of everyone's career. None of us are guaranteed anything in life, and even when we're seemingly on the verge of our greatest accomplishments, the rug can be pulled away at any moment.

With any setback in my career, I would put a limit on the time I spent processing those challenging feelings. For a serious injury I would give myself twenty-four hours. That's not to say I got over the disappointment of every injury within twenty-four hours – far from it, with something as major as this one – but that's the initial limit I put on this period where I really let it all out and just let go.

There are no hard and fast rules as to the time limit you need to set. For any leader there are setbacks of different scales. Failure to land an ambitious pitch you go for might be disappointing and require some time to grieve, just as losing a trusted lieutenant to a rival might, but certainly not as much as the failure of a business you have started yourself or a disastrous financial year. It's up to you to judge this – and it does get easier with experience – and also to know when you need those little extra pockets in which to deal with your feelings, especially when you're away from the team environment.

PARK IT, DUMP IT, DEAL WITH IT

After this time limit, you are then faced with a choice: park it, dump it, deal with it.

If you are able to dump it, then you can move on from this setback with relatively unchanged goals. This applies to milder setbacks – the minor injuries that involve a couple of weeks out, defeats in less-crucial games (though all defeats hurt to some degree), missed opportunities that don't have serious long-term repercussions. With some minor injuries I'd recover and never give them a second thought.

If you have to park it, it means you aren't yet ready to move on from the setback, just as I wasn't after my initial twenty-four hours following my injury. But you still have to go to work, turn up at the family table every evening or support your teammates. To do this, you build in windows for when you can close the door and let it all out again, and continue to process the setback while on the journey back to feeling 100 per cent. It's a cliché to say it, but time eventually does make this easier, and a strong personal purpose can be a real crutch during this time. There's a reason people 'throw themselves into their work' during times of crisis.

But you can't move on until you're ready to deal with it. Only once you are able to accept the reality of the new situation you find yourself in will you be able to move forward effectively. And this is where the power of a strong personal purpose and culture really comes to the fore. This is why your purpose has to be so strong, to connect with something deep within you and yet speak to something far greater than just yourself. In this instance it's a tool to get you over your setbacks and disappointments, so if you've arrived at a wishy-washy purpose that doesn't really connect, it's going to be more difficult.

My personal purpose, of course, wasn't just to be an All Black, but to strive to be an All Black great. When I originally aspired to this purpose, which I had been living for a number of years by now, I knew it was going to be a period of ten or more years, that I would need to work harder than my competitors. So, now, while in the midst of a setback, I asked myself, *What would an All Black great do?*

If I aspired to be an All Black great, then I knew I would need to rehab better than I'd ever rehabbed before to recover from the injury. I would need to work harder than anyone who has had an injury like this before. I would get the best specialist possible to help me. And I would have to reset my goals so that I could play at the next World Cup.

I thought 2011 was going to be my last World Cup, and I intended to go and play overseas afterwards, but all that had now changed. Thanks to that purpose I'd set for myself all the way back in 2003, I had some direction – a way to get through this situation. While my purpose remained the same, goals inevitably need to adjust along the way. In sport there are injuries and setbacks that will force them to change pretty quickly, just as there are things like redundancy, market forces and global financial crises in business and life, so it pays not to get too far ahead, though in this case working towards the next World Cup four years away as part of my personal purpose really helped me. At that time, injured and broken as I was, who knew if I was going to make it? But it helped me to move on with some direction for the next four years and get out of that vicious cycle of grief.

HOW CAN I HELP THE TEAM?

With a personal purpose pointing your way out of the disappointment, in a culture like the All Blacks, where **no individual is**

bigger than the team, you then need to look at how you can help the team. It's a strong personal value for me too, looking to help the greater good. And what that means is that I'm not going to just walk away from the team and go on holiday. I set out to help this team do something they hadn't done for twenty-four years. I'm now injured and unable to play, but how can I still help them do that?

There were young players coming into my position who needed help. Colin Slade initially, but he was then injured in the quarter-final against Argentina, which was a bitterly disappointing blow for him. Aaron Cruden then came in for him, but even he went off injured in the final and Stephen Donald came on to kick the winning points and secure us the World Cup in the tightest final in history, against France. The New Zealand World Cup hoodoo had apparently been replaced by the All Black fly-half hoodoo.

Being able to help these players even though I wasn't able to play on the field was a way to contribute. I wasn't pushing myself on these players; I was just letting them know I was around if they wanted to talk about anything and looking to help the team in any way I could. But it was tough. It really drained my energy because I was still dealing with my disappointment. Yes, I'd had my initial twenty-four hours to grieve, but it's impossible to simply flick a switch and imagine you can turn it all off, especially with a major setback.

With a more minor setback, I might have a brief period to process it and then never think about it again, but with a major one like this it's going to take time. I'm not a robot who can just turn my feelings off – it still hurt. When I returned to my hotel room after not being able to physically participate, I'd be upset but I'd use that time to process those feelings once again. However, once I walked out the door again the next day I'd know it was time to park those feelings for now and help the team again.

If you're moping around for weeks on end you can find yourself in trouble. It becomes harder to get out of that state the longer it goes on. You need to find windows where you can deal with your emotions – to let it all out – and then, using your 'now' focus and the mind-management skills we talked about in Chapter 4, switch back into dealing with what's next: *OK, what are my goals? What tools do I need today?*

What made this period doubly difficult was that as the team was progressing through the quarter-final, the semi-final and eventually the final to win the competition, my feelings of disappointment at not being a direct part of it were being magnified by the team achieving what we'd dreamed of together but without me on the field. I fed off the positivity of the team's achievements and being able to help in whatever way I could off the field, but I still needed those pockets of time to accept and process these feelings because it wasn't fair to share any negativity I was carrying in that environment. Winning a World Cup is hard enough as it is, and requires a singular focus, so my feelings were my own to manage (though, of course, I had some excellent support around me should I need it).

It's your ego you're dealing with as well as your disappointment. I've talked a lot so far about the team coming first, but it's natural to want to be out there contributing, to be a direct part of those winning moments, especially when you're used to playing a major role in the team. So when that's taken away it's incredibly hard to deal with. I don't believe it's human not to feel some sort of personal disappointment at these moments – ask any player who has missed a final because of injury or suspension and I suspect they will tell you the same.

When the team eventually won the World Cup at last it was an amazing moment. The sense of achievement, of *relief* in the side was incredible. And I have the fondest memories of sitting in the changing room at Eden Park after we'd won, taking it all in. It's so important to celebrate success, which I will discuss more fully in Chapter 10 (Sacrifice). And it's vital for this celebration to be inclusive, to involve everyone who has been pulling in the same direction on the team's journey towards its purpose: the support staff, the coaches, the backbone, the first team – and the injured, like me.

But I'd be lying if I said I didn't feel there was also something missing.

I felt so proud of the team, having seen the changes in the environment over the years. I'd been there in 2003, for the cultural reset in 2004 and for the bitter disappointment in the quarter-final in 2007. But I can't say I felt 100 per cent fulfilled by the 2011 victory. There was unfinished business for me. Call it ego, call it a selfish streak, but I believe any individual with high-performance aspirations – and whose purpose was so tightly aligned with their team's – would be thinking the same thing I was right then: *This is going to be me in four years' time.*

THE LONG ROAD BACK IS PAVED WITH SHORT STEPS

After the World Cup, when the team had achieved its goal and we all went our separate ways, it would have been easy to sink into despair. With no responsibility to the team to keep me going it would have been easy to relax and take refuge with my dark thoughts. But this setback, easily the worst of my career, gave me the motivation to drive forward after the World Cup.

Like anyone who has lost a major deal, been passed over for promotion, let go from a company, failed in business or messed up in their own lives, I had no idea what the future would look like. Who knew then how long my body would last or whether a younger player would come through and take my place. I couldn't control those things, so there was no point worrying about them. But I do know that, following an injury, I can control things like how much effort I put into rehab, what I eat and how I communicate with my coaches, so my energy needs to be concentrated on those things.

When you're dealing with any kind of setback, learning to focus only on what you can control and throwing all your energy into that is the key to making progress. So, while you obviously do have to learn from setbacks, spending too much time thinking, *I wish I'd done that differently,* or becoming overly concerned about a rival potentially usurping you just isn't going to help. Again, this is where acceptance can play such a big part. If you have been able to accept the reality of your situation, instead of continuing to question it with what-ifs or being in denial for too long, then you're going to be able to focus more intently on what you can control.

Ultimately, though, it comes back to the mind control we've talked about in the last couple of chapters. Throughout my career, the first thing I would do when I woke up on the morning of the game was to get up and open the curtains to see what the weather was like. I never stopped doing it, but what did change was my reaction to what was out the window. As a young player, if I opened the curtains and saw howling wind and rain, my immediate reaction would be, *Oh, man, how am I going to kick goals in that?* It wouldn't matter that it was exactly the same for the opposition, nor that the game wasn't until later, in the evening (and the weather in New Zealand can be very changeable anyway, especially in places like Auckland), I would waste time and energy worrying about the one thing none of us has any control over: the weather.

What happened later in my career was that I learned to manage it. I'd still open the curtains, and if I saw howling wind and rain my heart would still sink. But then the first step would be to recognise it, and the second would be to bring my focus to something I could control. I would do simple things like have a shower, get breakfast or write some pre-game notes in my book. Having a structure in place for your day really helps with this, of course, and so does the work Gilbert Enoka did with me on mapping out my next twenty-four hours, concentrating on what's next. Because worrying about kicking in the match is worrying about the outcome – it's not dealing with the things I can control in the now. The thing I can control is the process – so I get on and do that.

Back in 2011, I knew I could bring my work ethic, experience and developing ability to deal with setbacks to bear – living in the now, focusing only on what I could control, accepting my situation – which would prove key to getting through the next four years. With the next World Cup just four years away, my ultimate goal, I needed to look at the process and structure. You can't just focus on a four-year plan, there are too many potential pitfalls along the way. You need to start with the here and now. *What does the next year look like?* I would then start breaking the year down and setting goals, with the aim to be back on top by the end of the year. *So, what is my next competition? The Super Rugby season, for the Crusaders. I need to play well in that competition. How do I do that? I have to rehabilitate well.* After you have your goal in sight, then you have to look at what the next week looks like and structure that, down to the day, in order to work towards it. You have to look at how you're going to get the best out of that day – how am I going to make sure that I rehabilitate better than the day before? These days, then weeks, then months are all stepping stones towards the greater goal, but it is only through focusing on this process *right here, right now* and keeping your mind off the outcome that you can hope to get through it.

Looking forward to the World Cup four years away isn't going to help. It's only going to feel daunting and so far away it becomes abstract, unknowable. But by looking at the next twenty-four hours and saying I'm going to do this to the best of my ability, to focus all my energy simply into *what's next,* the task becomes more manageable, tangible. *Realistic.* And you have your markers along the way, the goals you reach and achieve that keep your motivation burning: returning from injury, playing well for the Crusaders, getting picked for the All Blacks, helping the team win each game, each series.

Towards the end of 2012, I won the World Rugby Player of the Year award for the second time. Bouncing back from the dark, post-injury mindset of that hotel room in Wellington to winning that within the space of twelve months is something I'm hugely proud of. Whether I deserved that award or not – and there's still a part of me that thinks maybe I didn't – is for other people to debate. For me, the award served as a marker that I was able to get back to the top after two such serious injuries.

I think a level of maturity definitely helps with recovering from setbacks. An injury setback and six months out of the game in 2003, when I was a young player, probably wouldn't have felt like the end of the world and I'd be able to bounce back easily. I might have felt different a few years later with a few successful seasons under my belt, but again I'd probably have brushed it off. But these things would likely have stored up trouble for the future, because I wouldn't have used my time to grieve and then built the best structure to return. You need a degree of maturity to deal with your emotions, to process what's happened and how you feel.

SURVIVAL MODE

My first year on the road to recovery culminated in my World Rugby Player of the Year award and one of my better performances in the black jersey, against Scotland. But the following year, 2013, was probably my worst as a professional player, a vicious cycle of recurring injuries during which I would doubt whether I even wanted to continue playing professionally. I spent a lot of that year thinking, *Maybe it's time to retire* . . .

That year it felt like my body was just giving up on me. I couldn't string more than a couple of games together without being knocked out by another injury. I'd work hard to come back from a torn hamstring only to injure my calf after I'd recovered. Come back from that and then I'd need an ankle cleanout. It was relentless; I was really battling hard just to get on the field, let alone play to anything like the level I'd managed the previous year.

With each new setback I would have my time to grieve and then try to return to my purpose, my goals. But it was incredibly difficult to then be derailed a short time afterwards by a fresh injury, a new setback. I'd talk to Honor all the time about it. 'I think I'm done,' I'd say. 'No. No, you're not,' she'd reply. I'd wake up the next day with a new lease of life, determined to get through this, my purpose and goals clear in my mind. And then the next day I'd plunge back to the depths, seeing little hope for my future other than retiring because my body was giving up on me.

My mind was playing games with me, and the only way I found to deal with it was to switch to survival mode. To borrow another sport as an analogy, you're like a tennis player being overwhelmed by a superior opponent – you're just chasing and getting the ball back over the net to keep you in the point without even thinking beyond that. You're just trying to stay in the game. I would find it hard to get out of bed some days, knowing what lay ahead, the rehab, the little exercises that seem infinitesimal in the grand scheme of things. But every day I would force myself up, grinding my way through them at times, but doing them nonetheless. Keeping myself in the game.

HOW STRONG ARE YOUR SURVIVAL SKILLS?

Survival mode is just as important in any walk of life. You might be dealing with a series of personal and/or professional setbacks, when the last thing you feel like doing in the morning is getting up, logging on and facing your colleagues. The client dinner you have that evening might fill you with dread. Your setback might even involve you being out of work, waking each morning with the whole day looming dauntingly before you. But you've got to stay in the game. You've got to get up and log on. You've got to put your game face on for the client dinner and *just get through it*. You've got to get up, get dressed, look for the next opportunity – even if it just feels like going through the motions. Because the level of your performance isn't what's important here – it's the fact that you're turning in a performance at all, despite what you're up against, despite that voice inside your head telling you to give in. It's when you give in to this, when you decide to stay away from work, cancel the client dinner or just turn over and stay in bed all day that problems can really begin to snowball. You're not surviving then – you're in freefall, and you may need help to get you out of it.

Your purpose and your goals provide focus, but you have to lose yourself in your process, whether that's through rehab or training, or working through your to-do list, turning up to meetings or staying on top of your inbox, to keep your mind from feeling overwhelmed by just how far away you are from those goals. Sometimes you have to just survive. On the occasions when I returned to fitness and played, the last thing on my mind was playing well. It was simply getting through it, *surviving* without getting another injury, without having my body fail on me.

I was the tennis player simply chasing the ball down and shovelling it over the net in the hope of staying in the point. But once you become more used to survival, once you're on surer footing in the rally, you can start thinking about hitting your shots more constructively. Just as if you've been able to stay in your own game – just getting through the next piece of work, the next meeting, sometimes even just turning up every day and getting through it – you will eventually work through it and reach a point where you're able to perform to a level more befitting of your abilities.

The following year, 2014, I didn't play a lot of rugby, and the 2015 Super Rugby season was all about survival. Initially, my thoughts were, *Just try to get through sixty minutes.* Then as I became fitter and stronger, *Just get through the whole eighty minutes of the game.* By the time the halfway point of the season came around, I realised I'd got through a run of seven or eight games unscathed. My thoughts now were more along the lines of, *Well done, you're still in one piece.*

I hadn't been thinking about *how* I was playing, whether I was producing good rugby or not. It had been pure survival. But now that I had those games under my belt, now that I'd *survived*, I could look towards the second half of the season and start thinking about playing well, applying myself for the good of the team. *You can stop being selfish,* I said to myself – and to a degree survival mode on a personal level is selfish, because you're just trying to drag yourself through it; you don't have much capacity beyond that (though that's not to say teams don't have to operate on survival mode sometimes either – just hanging in there to stay in the game). But I could now start giving to the team, in what was my last year playing for the Crusaders.

Thankfully I started to get back to some sort of form and momentum, which was so important for the start of the international calendar. Any thoughts of retirement had been banished. I still wasn't sure if I'd be on a plane to England for the Rugby World Cup later that year, but I felt I was moving in the right direction. It was a goal that no longer seemed quite as out of reach as it had during the worst days of my rehab. But none of this would have been possible without that period of just hanging in there and surviving.

SETBACKS CAN BE A LEARNING OPPORTUNITY – AND A CHANCE FOR GROWTH

'Never waste a good crisis' goes the saying, and at some point after a setback, there needs to be a review, in which some tough questions must be addressed: *What was the cause of it? What can we learn from it?*

After our World Cup exits in 2003 and 2007, we explored the reasons why we lost, absorbed the lessons that could be learned from the experience, and took the growth we achieved as a result into the next tournament (much more successfully after 2007's defeat, of course). After every match we lost we would look at why, and what we could learn from it. Each time I was injured I would conduct a similar review. Sometimes, such as with my injury at Perpignan, the why would be clear – I'd been overworking my body – and the lesson similarly clear-cut: I needed to factor in some proper recovery time between seasons.

And sometimes, such as my efforts to rationalise my World Cup heartbreak, there isn't necessarily an answer to the cause: it's just a freak occurrence. And yet growth can still be achieved as a consequence: my change in direction still came out of this setback, ensuring I would target one more World Cup.

Setbacks are inevitable in any environment, sports and business alike. But if you aren't failing sometimes, it means you aren't playing hard enough. It's only by having the courage to challenge our own capabilities, to reach beyond where we *know* we can go, that we can hope to do great things – but at the same time risk failure.

As long as we're able to absorb the lessons from these setbacks and put them into practice, we have no need to fear them. History is full of those who failed, often many times over, before they succeeded. Steve Jobs was fired from Apple before he returned to lead the company he co-founded. Oprah Winfrey was fired from her job as a television reporter early in her career before she became the one-woman industry she is today. Lionel Messi was a losing finalist in the 2014 football World Cup before he came back eight years later to win it at his fifth World Cup.

These experiences all hurt at the time, but we learn from our defeats and find the opportunities for growth. I know that there are few darker places in rugby than the changing room immediately after a defeat. But I also know that once you get through that, you start having conversations about the game, with your teammates, the coaches. Sunday sucks, but then you look to the week ahead. And I know that, in an environment like the All Blacks, there's going to be that little bit of extra needle in training. There's going to be an edge to proceedings – and often in successful teams recreating that edge can be the hardest thing to do every week. We'd learn the lessons from our defeats and then we'd use this to deliver a response in the following game. I'd hate to be in an environment where we lost a game and nothing changed in our approach the following week. There has to be a response to setbacks, and an acceptance that at the heart of the Art of Winning, there are a good few losses in there too.

CAN YOU ABSORB THE LESSONS OF DEFEAT?

When you experience your own setbacks, it's vital to learn why they happened and how you can do things differently next time. More often than not, we instinctively know what we've done wrong and can begin to work out what we've learned, but not always, which is why external feedback is a crucial part of this development and understanding.

In sport we're fortunate in that we have video footage and coaches who can take us through any errors we're making during a match – things we might not even realise we're doing. You're going to need to ask for feedback from your own setbacks, so you can use an outside perspective – this applies to that unsuccessful interview, botched report or surprising review at work – as well as your own. Be sure, always, to ask for constructive feedback that will potentially highlight things you've missed.

Once you have the reasons why, you can then work on addressing them. Again, in sport we have our playing coaches, physios and mental skills coaches to guide us through coming back from a setback, whereas in your own career it might require some guidance and support from your manager or a colleague – or perhaps a mentor or coach, some form of talking therapy or other outside help.

It's worth any leader asking themselves, *Is there a way we can build external feedback into our team?* You might not have a video analyst, but a mentor or coach could offer their own version of an action replay of your own blind spots: it could be the way you deliver (or receive) challenging feedback, your body language over video calls or even the tone of your emails. Useful, objective feedback that will help you address minor errors or patterns of behaviour that you're not even conscious of doing.

Crucially, the onus to absorb the lessons of defeat is on you, on your ability to take these lessons and improve on them. It's almost like when we try something new out in training. We would have an idea for a play, test it in training and then if it fails there is a review, the lessons learned are incorporated and we either discard it or try a new version, which is tested once again. We wouldn't just try the same tactic again and expect different results, which is why it's crucial you absorb the lessons of the setback before you go again.

THE SIX STAGES OF BOUNCING BACK

As I lined up with my teammates before the 2015 World Cup final at Twickenham, I didn't really have time in the moment to appreciate just what it had taken to come back from that personal setback in 2011. Instead, I was filled with the certainty that we were going to win. There just wasn't any doubt in my mind. That might sound arrogant, but it isn't meant with any disrespect to that very good Australia team we were up against that day. It was just a feeling that, as I looked left and right at my teammates, and as I thought about what we'd been through together, the shared experiences and the culture we'd grown, our collective purpose to strive to be the most dominant team in the history of world rugby – an ambition that would continue long after this match – we would create history that day.

My feeling proved to be a reliable one. We won the World Cup and I had the fairy-tale finish to my All Black career. It was such an incredible end to that journey, one that I could scarcely have dreamed possible back in the changing room at Eden Park in 2011.

But would any of it have happened that way if I'd been able to play my part in the World Cup win in 2011? Would I even still have been an All Black by then if 2011 hadn't ended in such disappointment? As I said at the beginning of this chapter, I wouldn't be the man I am today without the setbacks and disappointments in my career. The desire to reach that World Cup in 2015 was what kept me going through the dark times of 2013 and 2014, even though there was no guarantee I'd get there. But as with any purpose, it's not the getting there that counts, it's the *striving* for it. Nothing is guaranteed, but the mental resilience I acquired throughout this time, even as my body proved anything but resilient, is a skill that endures to this day.

The process I went through to overcome that setback in 2011 is a process that I used throughout the rest of my career whenever I suffered an injury and is one that, even today, I still find useful to overcome setbacks of any kind. This is it:

1. Make time to grieve – get help if you need it.
2. Park it (build in further windows to process your feelings), dump it (for relatively minor setbacks only) or deal with it (move to 3).
3. Accept the reality of your latest setback, so that your approach comes from a positive mindset (while also building in those windows to process your feelings, if necessary).
4. Return to your personal purpose to give you direction and reset your goals according to the new reality you find yourself in.
5. Focus on what you can control: put in place the structure to help you achieve your goals and then lose yourself in the process of *doing* it.
6. Review. Ask yourself, *What can I learn from this setback?* This might come to you immediately after the setback or later – but put the lessons learned into practice.

I've found to my cost that success in any discipline is never guaranteed – it can never be taken for granted, and failure is the very real risk we take on when we attempt anything beyond our comfort zone. But I've also learned that these setbacks can build resilience and inspire future success provided we can manage them in the right way. I don't believe I would have been a World Cup winner in quite the same way without my experience in 2011, just as I believe our collective setback in the 2007 World Cup drove our success in the 2011 tournament. And in both instances, it was the management of the mental side of our lives and our game that enabled us to triumph. And if you want to experience similar triumphs in your own life, it's this mental strength that must be developed.

THREE POINTS - RESILIENCE

1. The road to success is paved with setbacks: learn to accept that they're part of the journey.

2. Make time to grieve. Then find pockets of time to process your negative feelings when you need to.

3. Sometimes it's just about staying in the game: getting out of bed each day, putting in a shift at work. Survival mode won't last for ever.

There needs to be an acceptance that feedback is being given *for the good of the team.* You challenge each other, you debate things, all for the good of the team. But you play the ball, not the man.

CHAPTER 7

MAKE YOURSELF HEARD

My time with the All Blacks coincided with that of someone I consider to be the greatest ever to pull on the black jersey: Richie McCaw. He led us to back-to-back World Cups. He became All Black captain at the age of only twenty-five. After the crushing blow we suffered at the World Cup in 2007, he became like Michael Jordan in *The Last Dance*. Totally motivated, completely focused, fixated on greatness. Not his own greatness, though. It was always about the team's.

I've joked before that I lost my mate for a while after 2007 because he was so focused on putting right our loss to France and making the All Blacks World Cup winners in 2011. But I'm only half-joking. Nothing was going to get in his way. His dedication and leadership were an inspiration to us all, and we all wanted to do our best to support him on our journey together.

Richie McCaw is, by anyone's metric, a great leader. He is so driven, so determined – but what really stood out for me when we played together was his actions. The number 10 and number 7 (Richie's number) play quite close to each other, so I was able to witness first hand just how much he put his body on the line for the team. There was nothing he'd ask of someone that he wouldn't have been prepared to do himself. There was no bullshitting with him, he was full of integrity – if he said he'd do something, he did it – and he always put the team first. Crucially, it was a combination of all these things that allowed him to *consistently* deliver. It was that consistency which made him such a great leader: he never seemed to have an 'off' week or a day or two when he might cruise; he was working to a world-class level at everything he did, every time.

Leaders like Richie are a rarity, though. Most of us don't have an innate talent for leading. I, for one, was certainly not born to lead. I had to learn how to do it. I was a shy country boy when I first entered the All Blacks environment. I wanted to be an All Black great, not a great All Black captain. I kept pretty quiet, just trying to do my job, to start with. But what I discovered over the course of my career is that leadership is a skill that can be grown and developed. In fact, the best leaders are those that learn and develop over time – even the likes of Richie, who would be the first to agree with that. Although the captain of the team has the official title, leadership doesn't rest on his shoulders alone.

In the All Blacks culture we had created, we were all encouraged to embrace the opportunity to be leaders. Richie was the captain, of course, but in any strong organisation you need leaders all over the team. You need people who can make good decisions, remain calm under pressure, communicate well, build strong relationships, and offer challenging feedback that importantly *isn't taken personally.*

We had our leadership group, of which I eventually became a part, but crucially we had a culture where players were empowered to have responsibility – to deliver the game plan, to police the standards and crucially to lead ourselves and make decisions on the field. Empowering your people to do that is one of the key responsibilities of any leader.

THE IMPERFECT 10

When I first came into the All Blacks environment, it was as an inside centre, the number 12 (what we call a second five-eighth in New Zealand). It's an important position in the team, playing next to the fly-half (or first five-eighth), but it doesn't have the same level of responsibility for the overall attacking strategy of a team. A number 12 needs to know his role within the backs and support the number 10, but he isn't orchestrating play in the same way as the number 10.

That suited me fine at the time. I thought then that it was the captain's job to do the speeches and, as a young man adjusting to life in the All Blacks environment, I was quite happy to sit back and be comfortable. But all that changed on the 2004 tour that marked the beginning of the cultural reset that our coaching team had implemented, when our star number 10s – Andrew Mehrtens and Carlos Spencer – weren't picked and I was told I'd be playing in the number 10 jersey for the All Blacks.

I was excited to be given the opportunity, of course, but I also felt a new sense of pressure. It simply wouldn't do to be a quiet player in the team anymore, even if that's where I felt comfortable. The number 10's role in the team involves knowing when the team should run with the ball and when it's time to kick. The 10 leads the attacking strategy and calls the moves for the backs. They decide what the right play is for that moment. A good number 10 is a leader, has to be decisive and well prepared, and absolutely needs to speak up.

It was time to step up and embrace the pressure, walk towards the challenge. It wouldn't be enough to simply know my role and do it as well as I could, I needed to know the game plan better than anyone else; I had to understand the roles of every other player in the team because I would effectively be directing them at times. I'd have much more homework to do: as well as ensuring that I nailed my own role first, I then had to learn what everyone else was doing around me. I'd need to know what the loose forwards' role would be after each scrum. I also needed to know things like where we were planning to attack off the lineout and exactly who would be cleaning out at that first breakdown.

But I'd definitely need to improve my communication. I quickly learned that it was one thing having the knowledge, but quite another delivering it for real. I had a habit of speaking too quietly or mumbling. I struggled for confidence in my delivery, and I knew I couldn't just expect to turn up when the moment came and expect that everything would be OK without proper preparation. I had to practise and train for it.

During training I would exaggerate my communication. I

would make it much louder and enunciate more than I was comfortable with, really turning the volume up so much that some of my teammates looked at me as if to say, *What on earth are you doing? We're not deaf!*

But I knew that in the pressure of a real Test match environment, I'd revert to what came naturally. So I kept at it, making a conscious effort to exaggerate it. Much like the training we would later do in dealing with pressure situations, I would communicate far louder than would be required in the Test match environment so that come game time, when the noise from the crowd makes communicating even more difficult, I would be comfortable with what was required of me.

CLEAR, PRECISE, DIRECT COMMUNICATION

What I learned most of all as I developed my role as the number 10 in the team was that communication in any environment needs to be clear, precise and direct. Talking for the sake of talking is terrible communication. I've seen people shunted into a leadership role and they suddenly seem to think they have to just keep talking, as if that's what's required of a leader. It just doesn't work when you're in a position where instant decisions under pressure have to be made. It has to be:

- **Clear** – that the receiver is in no doubt what is meant.
- **Precise** – no wasted words, just the absolute essence, the headline.
- **Direct** – delivered to the right people at the right moment.

In order to ensure communication is direct, you need to work out what the lines of communication are. If you have fifteen messages from fifteen people on the field it just makes for confusion, which is why you need a leadership group and leaders in key positions. When communication is required, you're looking for the leaders in certain roles to communicate, and the route to this is through the micro-conversations each group is having on the field.

So, for example, the players in the front row – the props and the hooker – will be constantly talking and adjusting as the game goes on. That level of constant talk and detail is important to them, but as a player in the backs I don't need all of their information. I do, however, need some of it – which is where the leader there comes in. It's up to him to decide what information to share for the good of the team, and what isn't important. In a sense they're acting as a filter, as part of the lines of communication during a Test match.

As a leader in any organisation, you need to have a good line of communication with the key people necessary to your role. One of my most important lines of communication was with the captain, and I made it my mission to be Richie's go-to man. That's why people watching us play would see a lot of us working together, talking to each other. He was the one communicating directly with the referee and making decisions about what we did from penalties, so I needed to liaise with him to make sure everything was aligned between us and the decisions I was making were in the best interests of the team. Richie was the kingpin of the team, so I needed a good line of communication with him.

The next two big ones I needed to focus on were the two positions next to me on the field. Number 9, the scrum half (or halfback), is a position I played a lot as a young kid, because I was so small. I know that the number 9 is going to have his head down, the ball in front of him, while he controls the forwards. I know that I'm his eyes: he shouldn't be looking for me – he should be *hearing* me. If he looks up he might miss the ball coming out. It meant my job was to constantly talk to him, but that doesn't come about without putting the work in.

I would spend time with the number 9 on the training pitch working on our communication, of course, but also time off the field, talking things through, getting to know each other and what would help us communicate as effectively as possible on the field. And once you're on the field, it's loud and there's lots going on, so you have to make sure your communication is direct. Aaron Smith, whose nickname was Nuggy, played number 9 in the latter part of my All Black career. I'd say, 'Nuggy, I'm deep' or 'Nuggy – hot, hot, hot!' which means a quick ball. It sounds a simple thing to state, but as soon as he hears his name in the cauldron of noise he knows he needs to tune in. When there's so much going on, your mind needs something to hook on to and filter out the other noise.

The next important line of communication for me was with my number 12, who was the eyes and ears for me. I can't see what's happening out on the wing, so it gets relayed in by the number 12. Ma'a Nonu usually played this position during my time, and he understood the importance of helping the number 10. He really developed his lines of communication and his growth was second to none. Again, we worked on this off the field as well. It takes time to build a rapport and establish an understanding.

This communication became key in a Test match. We might be working the ball out wide and then getting tackled. 'What are you seeing behind the line?' I'd ask Ma'a. I can't see it, so I'm relying on him. He might then tell me the opposition full-back is coming up, so I know there's space there. Throughout a Test match, you're constantly learning and communicating, constantly building a picture about the game through your own observations and the information being communicated to you.

As a number 10, I'm effectively arming myself with information in order to execute the right strategy to win the game. We might go into a game expecting the opposition to defend in a certain way, and then throughout the game I'll get confirmation from the players around me and from what I'm seeing that they either are or aren't. It's like a game of chess, in which I spend sixty minutes trying to figure it all out and then spend the last twenty pulling the trigger and executing the right strategy to unlock their defence.

We took real pride in finishing teams off in the last twenty minutes. Earlier in the game the opposition is pumped up and coming at you, and you have to absorb that pressure – but all the while you're learning from it, working out any weaknesses, probing for where the space is. You can't cover an entire rugby field with fifteen players, so there has to be space or opportunity somewhere – you just have to work out where. If you get to eighty minutes and you still haven't figured it out, it often means you've been outfought and outplayed by your opposition and you've lost.

WHO ARE YOUR EYES AND EARS?

No leader can be everywhere at once, so you have to have good lines of communication with other leaders and departments throughout your organisation. Who is your number 12, feeding you the information about what's happening out on the wings? Who is your number 9, directing the people in front of you as you seek where the next opportunity will be? Ask yourself if you're communicating enough – your clear, precise and direct communication should be constant, so that you have the clearest picture possible.

UNDER PRESSURE: CLEAR, PRECISE, DIRECT

I've worked with some truly brilliant communicators throughout my playing career. I would reach a point with some players where we didn't even have to talk to each other on the field to communicate – we'd just give each other the eyes or a look and know that a certain move or pass was on. There are no shortcuts to this almost 'telepathic' understanding – it comes from playing many games together and getting to know each other well.

When I was playing in Japan for Kobe Steelers, the Australian player Adam Ashley-Cooper was on another level with his clear and direct messaging, an absolute joy to play with. Conrad Smith, our outside centre for the All Blacks, was another. But what all of these great communicators had in common was their ability to do it when the pressure was at its most intense.

You could be down by four points with thirty seconds to play, and Conrad's communication would be so calm and clear you wouldn't know if there were thirty seconds left to play or thirty minutes. I've played with other guys, however, who in the same situation would have found themselves with their hearts pounding, speaking quickly and frantically, pushing their anxiety and pressure onto the rest of us.

As with anything at the highest level, it's how you deal with it under pressure that can make the difference between winning and losing. You need to be in the now, to focus on the process. You will always have periods when you go into a red state, but you need to pull yourself out as quickly as possible. You need to breathe, of course, but I also had those three key communication touchstones to call on when the pressure mounted: *Clear, precise, direct* was my mantra, my process for communication.

As I said earlier, when I started playing you could get away with being one of the quieter ones, without being a skilled communicator. But the game moved on so fast during my playing career that the expectation became that everyone had to have the ability to communicate what they're seeing in order to help the team.

Often when guys went quiet it was because the pressure was on and they were in a state of red. It was a surefire way to tell if I was. So I learned to communicate to try to help them out of it. Ask them simple questions such as, 'Who's tackling you?' 'What can you see?' Just talking to them, getting them to focus on the next task, the next process and get them out of the red.

Players inadvertently communicate the fact that they're in the red all the time. The 'fight' response is usually easy to spot, and body language often betrays people when they have all sorts of things running through their mind and distracting them from what's happening *right now*. The opposition can see this too. Quite often it's easy to spot when your opponents are in the red, which is where focusing on your body language can help you through this. If you're able to control your mind, get out of a state of red, and stand up looking strong, the opposition will have no idea about what's going on in your mind. It's a skill from competitive sport that can be applied to any walk of life, and it's particularly important in the workplace, where things like your posture and eye contact can help you project confidence and strength.

Good opponents will be talking to the ref calmly. They'll be geeing each other up, patting each other on the back – generally giving off the impression of having plenty in reserve. On the other hand, if you look at your opponents with five minutes to go until half-time and they have their hands on their knees, puffing, and arguing with the referee, you know you've got them. Their communication breaking down is a surefire tell that they're struggling, and we were always looking for signs of that.

We would always do our best to fake it if we were feeling in a similar way. If it's five minutes till half-time and you're already exhausted, you don't show it. You sprint off to the changing room at half-time as fast as possible, because no one can see you there recovering. We'd make a point of beating the opposition to the changing room at half-time. You see a lot of teams taking their time, walking slowly and taking a breath, but not the All Blacks. Not the Crusaders. You can have your breather in the changing room – the important thing is to communicate the fact that you're still full of energy and ready for more.

It was definitely a period of adjustment, but I improved greatly in my communication through being in a leadership position in the team. Initially I was focused on being clear, precise and direct, but after 2007, the more confident I got as a communicator, the more demanding I became. It was a huge period of growth for this aspect of my game, allied to my elevation to the leadership group in the team. My language would become more along the lines of: 'Hey, I need you to tell me this. I need you to hit the ball on this angle next time!' I was demanding more of the players around me – demanding excellence.

In December 2015, after the World Cup and my retirement from the All Blacks, I played my first game for Racing 92 in France. My old teammate Joe Rokocoko was playing on the wing, and at the end of the game he came up to me and said, 'Oh, man, I've missed you bossing me around! I haven't had that for a long time!'

It was quite the turnaround from the introverted communicator I was at the beginning of my career, and I can put that down to the gradual accumulation of experience I acquired through being given more responsibility in the number 10 role and the player-driven culture we were building. It was good to hear those words from Joe, because I know not everyone feels the same about being directed on the field, and that's something that has to be managed.

FEEDBACK

In order to get to a point where you can be demanding of others and crucially maintain a healthy working relationship, you need to put in the hours off the field. If you work on these things off the field then they're not going to come as a surprise when you're on it.

Being demanding isn't the same as being grumpy or difficult; you're simply demanding the best from those around you. You have the best interests of the team at heart, so you need to be able to express these things in an environment of excellence without any unnecessary fallout. This means a purpose-led environment where the people drive the culture, where **no individual is bigger than the team** is a core value, and where it is accepted that *every* role is a vital part in the success of the organisation – and as such must be performed to the best ability possible.

So, if I'm being demanding of Joe Rokocoko in a match on the Saturday, we'll have a coffee in the week and talk about it. It might be that I've gone too far and he's not happy with what I was saying, in which case we can talk about it. It might be that

I need to apologise, to explain that I was in the red and I need to communicate more effectively next time. So you're always learning, always growing and changing the way you communicate with people.

These one-to-ones became known as 'relationship meetings', and we found that the team was at its best when a lot of these meetings were taking place. They were always very informal – just going for a coffee with a teammate – but they required an ability to deliver and receive challenging feedback at times.

At the start of my career, I would actively avoid having challenging conversations or relationship meetings. *No thanks*, I'd think. And, to be fair, it wasn't something that was particularly pushed back then. I was never comfortable challenging teammates. You'd often just let things slide. If someone was lowering the standards – being late to meetings or forgetting their book – I'd just let it go, and then later regret it. But as time went by this began to change.

If you want to strive to be the most dominant team in the history of world rugby then it's something you have to do. You have to be able to grow in all areas of the environment. At first if you're questioned and challenged by your peers, it's hard not to take it personally, to think, *Oh, he doesn't like me,* or maybe, *I'm not good enough for this environment.* But there needs to be an acceptance that feedback is being given *for the good of the team.* You challenge each other, you debate things, all for the good of the team. But you play the ball, not the man.

In a world-class environment, driving those world-class behaviours is the responsibility of everyone in it. Not just the captain, the coaches or the senior players – *everyone*. Delivering challenging feedback effectively is one of the hardest things you can do, and it wasn't something the team was particularly good at to start with. But we started by doing it in our leadership group, by trying to deliver and receive it without it getting too personal, and it became yet another of those things that got easier with practice.

The All Blacks values were of course ingrained in us, and in our team rooms we'd always be surrounded by these values and our purpose, so we knew that when you're having these difficult discussions, it's for the greater good of the team. But that didn't mean we didn't have to be careful with the way we delivered any uncomfortable truths. What I found helped when delivering challenging feedback was to approach the person concerned and ask for a chat – and to be upfront and clear what it was about.

'Look, Dan, can I have an uncomfortable conversation with you? It's nothing personal, it's just that what I'm seeing isn't for the best of the team,' is going to be better than something that sounds like an attack, such as, 'Hey, Dan, you're not living up to the standards – what's going on?' I found that this helped avoid anything confrontational, and then you'd sit down and have a one-to-one with them, explaining your thoughts and focusing on the issue rather than the person – playing the ball, not the man.

The person receiving the feedback might have no idea they've been falling short in some way, so it's always worth being prepared for the fact that it's news to them, and they might be able to explain why they've been behaving the way they have. Or they might dispute it and point to all the other things they're doing in the environment. It might even be that you've been pushing a bit of your own nerves or anxiety about something onto them, and the issue lies with you. But what's important is that you focus on the issue, have your conversation and then you move on, with some kind of resolution agreed on.

Again, acceptance is a major part of this: once you can accept that feedback is only being delivered for the good of the team, as part of a collective growth mindset in which the aim is to always improve, then it becomes easier to focus on the issue rather than taking anything personally. We got used to it, it gradually became habit, and it started to feed out into the wider environment. And trust me, if a team of huge, ultra-competitive, pumped-up rugby players can learn to give and receive challenging feedback then I'm confident anyone can – in the right environment.

And once you have an environment where people feel able to challenge their peers and deliver feedback, you know your culture is robust. You know that people are there to be the best they possibly can.

HOW THICK IS YOUR SKIN?

Building an environment where the giving and receiving of challenging feedback is an accepted part of the culture can be challenging. In the wrong environment – and even in the right environment sometimes – it can be difficult not to take feedback personally. And equally, it can be easy just to let things go, to not speak up and let standards slip, especially if you're the type who prefers to shy away from confrontation. So it's important that all feedback remains objective, works towards solutions and an outcome, and doesn't get too personal.

One way of doing this is by having a trusted moderator – a Gilbert Enoka type – to ensure things don't get too heated. And through getting used to delivering this objective, constructive feedback in such a manner, your people will eventually become able to do it peer to peer without the need for a moderator every time. There must be an acceptance that any feedback is being delivered to create improvement and to maintain the best possible standards. And crucially, feedback that you receive must then be acted upon. The solutions that come out of it aren't just words to pay lip service to – they're actions to be executed.

THE PLAYERS COMMUNICATE THE GAME PLAN

Leading into the World Cup in 2007, I took the next step up in my leadership journey by joining the leadership group. By then I was a more experienced player, with a couple of years under my belt of being the first-choice number 10 in the side and the extra responsibility that involved.

At first, I didn't contribute an awful lot to the group, to be brutally honest. I was twenty-five at the time, still relatively young, and I was a bit of a passenger. But I was listening the whole time and learning. And then, following the World Cup, experienced players like Leon MacDonald, Doug Howlett, Aaron Mauger and Byron Kelleher left and I felt like I was becoming one of the more senior players. That prompted me to step up again, and it was during this period, leading up to the World Cup in 2011, that I took a more prominent position in the leadership group. I made it my mission to be Richie's right-hand man and became his vice-captain.

Being captain of the All Blacks brings with it a lot of pressure. The entire country of New Zealand expects success, and the captain is the figurehead. But Richie was on such a drive to lead this team to greatness, to right what had gone wrong in 2007, that he put an incredible amount of extra pressure on himself. He was an inspiration to all of us, relentlessly setting the standards, but I think it's fair to say that he probably put a bit too much pressure on himself during the early days, carrying the weight of the team on his shoulders and dealing with everything himself. And one of the ways in which he developed as a leader was in his use of the leadership group. He learned to trust us and delegate more, which took some of that pressure off him. And once we were able to be of more help to him, Richie was able to lead to the best of his ability and we got the most value out of the leadership group.

The leadership group was simply a group of key leaders in the team, headed by the captain, and we would be the key drivers of communication with the coaches and implementing their strategy. The coaches saw it as their role to do the work on the game plan, but crucially that it was the responsibility of the players to deliver it. We were the ones who would be executing the strategy on the pitch, and they felt that by empowering us to take charge of the information, to know it inside out, we would not only have a better understanding of it, but also we would be able to make our own decisions on the field when things went wrong (which they inevitably do). We wouldn't be looking at them to ask, *What now?!*

So, we'd have a hierarchy of sorts when it came to communicating this information from the coaches. We'd have key drivers in key positions: my job was the attacking strategy and communicating this to the backs, but there'd also be someone in charge of the scrum, the lineout, the back three (the wingers and fullback) and so on. The coaches would give the leading players all the information, and it was our job to present it to the relevant people.

The first challenge for any of us absorbing all the information was knowing what to present to the team, which we'd work on with the coaches. Most of us in a rugby team are pretty simple folk at heart: we like clear, precise, direct messages to take out onto the field and execute. As soon as things become grey or muddled, open to more than one interpretation, then it can get confusing and people won't be aligned.

I quickly learned to keep it simple. Cover ten things and people might only remember a couple, but if you look at the critical two or three things to address and nail them, then you're in a much stronger position. I also learned the importance of knowing your audience. You don't need the front row worrying about the minutiae of the game plan – they have lots of other things to worry about, so they just need to know the headlines.

The leadership group served as the major line of communication with the coaches, but it's not like they just handed us the information and left us to get on with it. They would be keeping an eye out to make sure everything was on track, having micro-conversations during the week to make sure it was all sinking in. They were there, in the background, ensuring everything was going to plan, but empowering us to take it on.

TOO MUCH INFORMATION?

Of course, another role of the leadership group in the culture we had created was that we were able to challenge the coaches and offer feedback in that direction, as well as towards our peers.

The Hollywood image of any coach communicating with their players is one of a rousing pre-match or half-time speech that somehow spurs the players on to greater heights. Think Al Pacino in *Any Given Sunday*. The reality in the modern All Blacks environment is quite different, however, and that's in no small part down to our leadership group being able to challenge the coaches.

When he was first appointed, Graham Henry used to give these great speeches before we got on the bus to the game. But we increasingly felt we didn't need them: we were fully prepared and didn't need any rousing rhetoric to bring it come game time. Our captain at the time, Tana Umaga, eventually challenged him and said, 'What do we need these speeches for? We've done all the work, it's not making a difference. Are you doing it to get anxiety out?' Credit to Henry, who was a strong and decisive coach but open to constructive feedback from the players. 'If that's what you want then I'll stop,' he said, and there's never been a pre-match speech since.

Having an environment where anyone can be challenged and be open to feedback is a prerequisite for excellence. But it can go too far, sometimes: in some of the leadership meetings the coaches would definitely get a bit sick of us challenging their thoughts and debating things. However, what was absolutely paramount was that we'd debate things, and whether we all agreed or not at the end of it, we'd all commit to the course of action and move forward together.

One of the most poisonous things you can do in any team environment is debate, not agree and then all walk out of the room. You're not aligned and then you might go and talk to a couple of other players about what you thought, and that gets passed on by those players. The dissent spreads. But if you debate, commit and then talk to the other players about the decision you've all committed to, you can all walk forward together. There's no room in a winning environment for back-stabbing over decisions and players – dissent and discord spread like wildfire.

DEBATE, COMMIT, WALK FORWARD TOGETHER

With any meeting or disagreement, you *debate* the issue, and whether or not there is unanimous agreement you all *commit* to the resolution then *walk forward together*.

The coaches' roles also involve analysing the opposition and helping us through our review process. Our coaches did an enormous amount of work on the opposition – it's incredible how much detail they went into. In sport, if you don't trust the coach it's often because you don't think they've done the work. They might come up with a game plan and show you one little clip to demonstrate their point before they push the pause button. But it might not be a common trait – it might just be a one-off. Whereas the coaches I've worked with push the pause button but also have another ten clips to back up their point.

I'm often asked now, 'How much homework did you do on the opposition?' The truth is, I trusted the coaches so much that I didn't do a lot of analysis beyond what they showed me. Some players would be on a computer every spare minute they had, and it is a case of finding what works for each individual, but I think there's such a thing as too much information.

As the number 10 in the side I already had a lot rattling around my head: information from the players around me, the game plan, my preparation. Would spending three hours a week in front of a screen thinking about things the opposition *might* do, *might* bring to a game help? I spent the time instead refining my game, because I thought the opposition could bring anything and I'd be able to adjust or adapt. I'd prefer to work on things that would worry them in a game. I'd have a general idea of what the opposition would do from the coaches, of course, but I preferred to use my time to get better rather than worry about the opposition.

A GOOD REVIEW

While the coaches were empowering the players to take on responsibility, they also knew it was their role to manage us as individuals, which required different approaches for different people. Some players needed the heat on to get the best out of them, while others needed a bit more one-to-one time or a sympathetic arm around them. For any leader, this type of man-management is vital.

I needed to be challenged. I'd be questioned on decisions I was making, I'd debate things with the coaches. And at other times I'd be shown video clips of me playing. Our assistant coach Ian Foster was particularly good at this. We would have a talk, discuss how I was feeling and whether that married with what I was doing on the pitch. Were my intentions married to my actions? He was amazing at showing me clips of bad habits I was slipping into. I might be catching the ball and running sideways a bit but would be convinced that I'd been running dead straight before seeing the clip. *Right, let's work on that in the week.* To rectify it, I'd do little drills.

That's the beauty of a good review – it gives you a perspective you wouldn't get to on your own. At the end of a Test match, you walk off the field, do the media and then feel that you have a general sense about how the game went. *Oh man, we were awful today,* you might be thinking. Then you watch it back and review it, and you realise if we'd just done a couple of things differently it would have been a completely different game. It's not all doom and gloom after all.

Equally, the reverse can be true. You might walk off the field feeling like you've played a blinder, but when you watch it back you see that you're sluggish, slow off your feet. You see the stats and learn that the time you spent on the ground is higher than it has been all year. Your GPS numbers are off – you weren't as sharp as you thought that day.

I would go a lot off 'feel' in my career – I trusted my instincts and went with my gut on many occasions. But they were instincts that were honed through reviews, through feedback from coaches and teammates, through looking at the data. Instinct alone isn't enough – you have to look at all the means at your disposal to get the true picture of what happened, the best possible feedback. Quite often I would go off feel and then look for reassurance in the review, see if I was right. More often than not they married up, but certainly not always.

One thing the best coaches have in common is that the same approach every time isn't going to cut it. Different times call for different ways, and while I'd need to be challenged through various means in the environment, I was also a deep thinker – perhaps prone to overthinking at times. Sometimes you need to get away from that, and a coach like Steve Hansen, who was a genius when it came to knowing which approach to take, might take me for a beer, get away from rugby and take the pressure off my shoulders for a little while. A great coach knows when the right time for this is, because in the right environment they've got to know the person as well as the player. They'll see the signs you're communicating without you even realising that it's time for a change in tack.

CONTROL YOUR MESSAGE

When I finished playing rugby and was struggling to find a sense of purpose in my life, one of the things I found most challenging was when I was talking to people and they'd ask, 'So, what are you doing now?'

I didn't have an answer for that. I didn't want to tell the truth, which was, 'I'm just enjoying some time with my family.' I always felt that was not the answer they were hoping for. It would make me quite anxious whenever I sensed the subject was coming up – and it was killing me that I didn't have an answer that captured the same heights I reached as a rugby player.

When I met with Kevin Roberts, who as a former CEO of Saatchi & Saatchi knows a thing or two about communication, he told me that I just needed a one-liner to go to. A stock answer, if you like, that needed to draw a line under the subject while also being sufficiently vague and non-committal, given that I had no idea what I was doing next.

When people asked, I would reply, 'I'm repurposing my life so I can figure out how best to make a difference and make happy choices for my family and me.'

They'd say, 'Wow, that's really good.' And though they didn't say it, I could see them thinking, *What the hell does that mean?*

But that didn't matter. It gave me confidence, having that stock answer, and it showed me the power of owning my message while I got on with the work of actually working out what was next. During a period of change and uncertainty in anyone's life, it can be difficult to answer questions like these, which point directly at something we consider an issue in our lives. But by owning the message like this, by having a response we can go to each time, we can build confidence and dispel any wasted energy we might be using worrying about it – energy that would be better spent addressing the issue.

It's a lesson that felt especially true when it came time to let the world know I'd hung up my boots for good. On 20 February 2021, five months after I played my final match, for Southbridge, I officially announced my retirement. There had been a lot of speculation and rumours about what I was doing next, fake news that I was going to play in the US, and I'd had enough of it. By officially announcing my retirement, I finally drew a line under all that speculation.

Of course, in reality, it was one of the hardest things I've ever done: it's one thing committing to retiring in your mind, but quite another to share it with the world. You can't take it back then. But I didn't need to communicate the fact that I was moping around the house for days around the time of my announcement, mourning my playing days. I just needed to share the news in a clear, precise and direct manner, which I did on social media. I controlled the message.

CAN YOU CONTROL YOUR MESSAGE?

Good communication with your teams, your customers, your stakeholders or your wider industry are vital if your message is to be delivered the way you want it to be. If you aren't managing your message, then you're effectively allowing other forces to control it. You can draw a line under unhelpful speculation and rumours, or something that might negatively affect your organisation or team, and ensure your people feel well informed and included. Regular clear, precise and direct communication will allow you to step up and own the message.

THE DRUMBEAT

This final note about communication is one that could equally have opened the chapter, as it's possibly the most important aspect of any communication: *listen*. In a state of red, players often aren't listening, which means they aren't working to the game plan. Your communication can be as clear, precise and direct as you like, but if the receiver isn't listening, you're in big trouble. Make sure you're being heard. And make sure you're listening – really tuning in to what's being said – when someone's communicating with you. When presenting, ask questions of your audience to make sure people understand what is being said and that they're listening – that the information is going in.

Reid Hoffman talks about the 'drumbeat' a leader needs to set in an organisation, the rhythm by which your people all go together – what speed you're operating on, what you're doing and where you're going. It's the way everything is co-ordinated and synchronised in your organisation, and one of the ways to establish this, Reid explains, is by communicating a lot: 'You only begin to know you're communicating enough, once you get to a large organisation, when you're really tired of saying it. And at that point, maybe it's just begun to sink in.'

Businesses, just like sports teams, need constant communication to establish their drumbeat. They have their lines of communication, the filtering of knowledge by leaders throughout the organisation and the metronome of what it is they're doing and where they're going set by the ultimate leader in the organisation, just like the captain on the rugby field. There is constant communication to co-ordinate and synchronise with leaders in your organisation, and adjustment to changes in the market and in the face of what your competition is doing, just as on the rugby field I will direct the play, work with my captain to synchronise what we do next and adjust to what our opponents bring to the field of play.

Fast, efficient and constant communication is at the heart of any successful organisation, and anyone with leadership aspirations needs to be comfortable either setting the drumbeat or working in time to it. But as I hope I've shown, communication, like leadership, is a skill that can be developed and improved. Very few of us can be Richie McCaws or Reid Hoffmans, but we can all aspire to improve as I did and be the best communicator we possibly can, and ultimately the best leader we possibly can. And it all starts with that seemingly simple yet often most difficult part of all communication: *listening*.

THREE POINTS - MAKE YOURSELF HEARD

1. Keep your communication clear, so there's no doubt what is meant; precise, just the essential content required by the receiver; and direct, delivered to the right people at the right time.

2. Some of us are born leaders. Not many, though. Leading is a skill that can be developed like any other. Look at where you can make improvements.

3. Develop an environment where constructive feedback can be offered and received without being taken personally. Build thicker skins. Again, these are skills that can be developed through practice and eventually habit.

Change is often a result of circumstances, sometimes out of your control. And it is how you evolve as a consequence of those circumstances that determines whether you're going to be successful or not.

CHAPTER 8

STAYING AHEAD OF THE COMPETITION

EVOLUTION

In 2005, in the second Test against the British and Irish Lions, I had the match of my young life. I scored thirty-three points – two tries, four conversions and five penalties – a tally I would never match again in my career. There's no such thing as a perfect performance, but when I look back I think this is as close as I came to it, in my first year of playing number 10 for the All Blacks. And to do it in the series-deciding Test against the Lions, a chance that only comes round every twelve years or so, made it all the more special.

Fast-forward ten years, to the World Cup final at Twickenham in 2015, my last match in the black jersey. You could say, given that I was thirty-three at the time, I had the match of my autumn years (at least in sporting terms) as we won the World Cup final against Australia. I was named man of the match and scored nineteen points, all from my boot: four penalties, two conversions and a drop goal. It was the fairy-tale finish to my career, the moment I had been working towards all my life, and to cap it all with such a strong performance was incredible.

What is also incredible to me is that I was able to bookend my career with two such performances in two stunning team achievements. They are two very different performances. The first in 2005 that of an uninhibited, flamboyant young kid just playing with so much freedom and openness. I was on top of my running game, making line breaks and scoring tries, as well as kicking for my points. When I got to the changing room afterwards and received the flurry of messages of congratulations, I got a sense of just how special that performance was.

The 2015 game was different. You can see that in the way I scored my points, all from my kicking game. I wasn't the fleet-of-foot twenty-three-year-old playing without inhibition anymore – I had the physical and mental scars to prove that. But I did play with this sense of complete control. In fact, I'd never felt that I had so much control in a game before. It was a clinical number 10 performance. When we needed to change momentum in the match I was able to exert such control, and as the director of the play on the field it was an amazing feeling, a special performance that I'm extremely proud of. It felt like everything in my career had built up to that moment: my personal purpose and the team's, the highs and lows, the setbacks and fight-backs, the experience gleaned in ten years and over a hundred caps. To deliver such a controlled performance in those circumstances was the absolute icing on the cake for me.

It was the kind of performance there is no way I'd have

been able to deliver as a naïve young kid in 2005, just as I wouldn't have been able to play with the same flamboyance and freedom as I had then in the 2015 final. And that's simply because I had to *evolve* as a player with the challenges and setbacks ten years at the sharp end of international rugby had thrown at me.

This evolution was essential to my reaching 112 caps with the All Blacks. I realised very early on that it was a prerequisite for striving towards my personal purpose, *to be an All Black great*. Indeed, it was one of the four key qualities I identified when shaping my purpose all the way back in Chapter 1: *[An All Black great] Needs to constantly evolve his game and improve to develop as a player and beat off all challengers.*

I was able to win three World Rugby Player of the Year awards, at different stages of my career: the first in 2005, my breakthrough season; the second in 2012, following my post-World Cup injury lay-off; and the final one in 2015, my last season as an All Black. I was obviously proud to win these awards, but, as I've explained, they don't mean anything without your team around you. The thing I'm most proud of, though, is the fact that I didn't win all three of them in my first few years and just hang in there: I won them throughout my career, and to win one in my final year says to me that I was still on top of my game ten years after winning my first award. My longevity is a big source of satisfaction for me, but it was all down to my evolution as a player.

This process of evolution is what drove my leadership role within the team, as I developed from a quiet passenger into a key member of the leadership team. The game itself is evolving all the time. And evolution is as vital for a collective as it is for any individual. We evolved from a team unused to and unable to handle pressure at key moments to one that embraced pressure and walked towards it – from a team that hadn't won a World Cup for twenty-four years to the first ever to win back-to-back World Cups.

Because if you're not evolving, you're standing still. And if you're standing still, the competition can catch you up.

EXPERIENCE COUNTS
(BUT ONLY IF YOU USE IT WISELY)

Experience is a valuable asset in any discipline – but it often comes at a cost, particularly in sport. The youthful zip and flamboyance might diminish, that raw, explosive pace that characterised your early twenties might not be there in the same way in your early thirties. But how you're able to leverage your experience to create new strengths, rather than trying to compensate for old ones, is the key to longevity in any discipline. Legendary leadership coach Marshall Goldsmith devoted an entire book to this idea, *What Got You Here Won't Get You There*, in which he explained that the very strengths that allow us to ascend in the first part of our career can become weaknesses that cause us to plateau later on.

My bank of experience meant I was used to defences rushing up or defences holding back; loose forward trios targeting me; the open winger flying up trying to shut down our moves; the opposition back three all moving to try and challenge me to think where exactly the space is. There was nothing I hadn't seen in the game, which helped me adapt very quickly to any situation and speed up my decision-making. What I might have lost in speed over the years I'd made up for with the speed and quality of my decision-making. It sounds counter-intuitive, but playing the game felt easier.

Tom Brady, who is regarded by many as the greatest quarterback ever to play in the NFL, won his seventh Super Bowl at the age of forty-three. He has talked about how, having played for so long in the NFL, there isn't much he hasn't seen before from defences, which makes the game somehow feel easier.

It's the same for any experienced leader: they've been there, done that in a lot of situations, and through navigating the successes and crucially the setbacks and failures throughout their career, they will have the experience that, provided they're able to use it effectively, will allow them to make faster, more effective decisions, to lead in a way they know produces results. Their work will feel easier, even as their responsibility grows. They won't be doing as much of the 'leg work' that they did in their younger days, because their role has become one that now involves leading people, setting strategy, making decisions. The strengths that made them stand out in more junior roles and helped them to progress aren't necessarily the strengths that are going to allow them to thrive in a leadership role.

Only those that are able to bank their experience and lever-age it effectively will be able to make that progression – those that are able to evolve their approach, just as I had to evolve my physical preparation and, crucially, my recovery as an ageing athlete. And sometimes that means going back to the drawing board and starting all over again.

BACK TO BASICS

In 2014 I took a six-month sabbatical from the game. After the injury problems and dark hole I'd found myself in at times during the previous year, I knew drastic action was required if I was even to have a chance of making the plane for the World Cup the following year.

The picture-postcard highlights reel of my sabbatical included ticking a few things off my bucket list, like going to events that usually clashed with the rugby calendar: I went to the Augusta Masters, to Coachella music festival and to the Melbourne Grand Prix. I even went to Elton John's Oscars after-party. To the outside observer it might have looked like I was enjoying quite the glamorous lifestyle during my break from rugby. And don't get me wrong, I had a brilliant time at these events. But these short trips (and they were just a couple of days here and there) didn't even begin to tell the whole story.

This sabbatical was about putting my body back together. At the beginning, I sat down for a coffee with Pete Gallagher, the All Blacks physio, and Nic Gill, the All Blacks strength and conditioning coach, and we went through the list of my previous injuries, most of which they were pretty familiar with. And it was a long list. Then we talked about my goals, and this was pure short-term goal setting: I wanted to play to the best of my ability and help the team win the 2015 Rugby World Cup.

One more World Cup, I thought to myself. *That's all I want.* I didn't think about anything beyond the World Cup. This was all I needed. I definitely wasn't considering playing for another five years after that at this stage, and I knew I was by no means even guaranteed to be in the squad for 2015, let alone on the field.

Then we went across the road and did some baseline testing on my fitness. In the All Blacks environment, we did a lot of strength testing: How much can you bench press? How much can you squat? How many chin-ups with weights attached around your waist? What's your Bronco time? (A Bronco test involves shuttle runs of 20 metres then 40 and then 60, five times over.)

The tests Pete and Nic had me do on this occasion, however, were simply bodyweight exercises to work out where my weaknesses lay. And there were some exercises I couldn't even do. They didn't even have any weights on them! My right side was falling apart. From my glute down, it was relatively weak: my Achilles, hamstring, calf. I'd torn my left Achilles tendon, but strangely I'd done so much rehab on that side it was actually stronger than my right, my non-injured side, which is unusual. My right foot – my plant foot when I'm kicking – was being destroyed. There was all the wear and tear, scar tissue and all the damage I'd done through kicking thousands and thousands of balls. I'd had two operations on my right ankle, which was now super-stiff compared to my left, and I couldn't even get my knee over my toe when we tested how much flexion I had in my ankle. All of which meant my gait was out.

I was strong, I just wasn't strong in the right areas and my technique was poor because I didn't have the mobility or the flexibility. It was a bit of an eye-opener for me, not to mention a bit embarrassing not to even be able to do some of the exercises, but it didn't come as a huge shock to Nic or Pete. They'd seen it all before, and I think a lot of athletes are like I was then: you just don't usually have long pre-seasons to put all these problems right.

But I did now. I had the time to go back to the drawing board with my body. And, with a programme drawn up by the world-class team of Nic and Pete, who would check in with me regularly to monitor my progress, I began six months of some of the hardest training I've ever done. I had to go back to basics, starting with relearning proper technique for weight-lifting and building up the flexibility to do it right. I had to get my body aligned and in balance, instead of having one side strong and the other weak.

I had been used to 'pumping tin' in the gym, a whole load of testosterone fuelling our efforts to outdo each other in the team, so it was humbling to regress to the very fundamentals and relearn how to lift and exercise properly. But it was also exactly what I needed at that moment in time.

And that's key when it comes to evolving in any field. You have to do the work, of course, but you have to be humble too. Sometimes you have to embrace a beginners' mindset, even with something you think you already know how to do well, in order to evolve. I had to shelve my ego as a successful athlete and be humble enough to do the sort of exercises first-timers at the gym are doing. I had to commit to the process and trust that the outcome would take care of itself – and get my body to where it needed to be. In some ways it made me think about whakapapa, and how we first need to go back to where we've come from before we can walk forward.

When I spoke with Tim Brown, the New Zealand former footballer and now co-founder of billion-dollar footwear company Allbirds we met in Chapter 1, he told me about his transition from professional sport to becoming an entrepreneur. Tim has a philosophy about making these transitions throughout your life – no matter what field you work in. He thinks that, in your first career path, you make your way up to your peak in that discipline, and then every time you make a career transition, you come down from that peak to the foot of the next one. But crucially, you don't come down to the level you were at prior to your first peak because of the experience you have accrued. You're at a higher level – a base camp, if you like – with the potential for a higher peak the second time around.

So, I've had my first peak, working hard to reach the top in rugby and achieving success there. But now I've come down to the beginning of my next peak. But my next peak – much like that of anyone who has experienced one before – has the potential to be higher than the first, because of the experience I am able to bring to bear. And this knowledge can be reassuring, especially when you're in the middle of a change and you feel like it's a long road ahead. You're not back at the bottom; you're at the starting line of what's next.

Key to successfully scaling your next peak is this ability to embrace a beginners' mindset, to be humble enough to accept that you're at the beginning again and you need to learn new skills and start over. If you have scaled your first peak and are now in the middle of your own mid-career transition or period of repurposing, then you won't get far without the ability to shelve your ego, put to one side the achievements you accrued during your first peak and focus on the process in front of you. Your ascent will reach beyond the heights of the first – but only if you can do this.

The experience of rebuilding my body taught me a lot. I learned that it's OK to take a break when you've put your body and your mind through so much and for so long, just as long as you have aspirations *to come back stronger and better than before*. If you're doing it because you've lost your way and you're hoping to find the motivation afterwards, that's going to be tough. And again, this is where the power of a strong personal purpose comes in. I took that time off with real purpose and of course I had a tangible goal – just as if you're changing course in your career, you need a tangible goal to aim for, otherwise you can just drift. An All Black great rebuilds his body, does whatever it takes to come back stronger and give himself the best chance possible to play in the 2015 World Cup. It certainly wasn't six months 'off', despite what the picture postcards might have said.

TRAIN SMARTER, NOT HARDER

Another big thing I took from my sabbatical was the realisation that I was now an ageing athlete. I wasn't in my twenties anymore – I was a thirty-two-year-old athlete with a couple of hundred first-class games in a contact sport under my belt. My priorities needed to change a bit, just as they do in any walk of life when you realise that age is catching up with you. The things I was doing ten years ago were no longer the right things for me to be doing now.

So what, then, are my goals? To try and get a personal best on the squat machine or the bench press? Those days are gone. But how about getting your personal bests out on the rugby field on a Saturday instead? So instead of trying to outwork my teammates in the gym, something I'd once prided myself on, I was doing more work on specific muscle groups and doing a lot of little exercises to get the important muscles firing, which would help prevent injury and give me more chance of getting out on the field. I was looking for new ways to look after the key asset in my career. I was making an investment in my body.

Back in 2011, when I tore the adductor muscle from my pubic bone and my World Cup ended, I spent a lot of time asking, *Why?* It was such a freak injury. I never really got to the root of why it happened, but one thing I did wonder was whether I was maybe spending a bit too long working on my six-pack for the beach (and Jockey shoots), and not doing a lot of the deep inner core work. So I started doing Pilates as part of my rehab, which is fantastic for working on those deep core muscles. It was just a different way for me to train. Before, I'd do my sit-ups and banded core work at the end of a gym session and think that was enough. But that injury showed me that there are other ways to do it that are less strenuous on the body. And it soon became a huge part of my weekly routine, which I continued through my sabbatical.

I also learned to make time for myself. When you live such a busy life, things can play inside your mind in terms of the expectations or the media that you have to do, being a public figure. You actually just need time to yourself, and I made sure when I was on tour in particular, because you're always around the team, to regularly take ten minutes to myself. It was like meditation. I would just work on my train of thoughts, trying to clear my mind. I had some meditation apps that helped me with that, and just taking some time away to control my thoughts and control my brain was another part of my routine near the end of my career.

When I was younger, my day off was my day off. For the first five or six years of my career, I would use my day off to get away from rugby, to have some fun. Whereas nearer the end of my career it wasn't a day off. It was a recovery day. So I'd go to the pool, do some Pilates, jump on the compression machine, have an ice bath, go for a massage – whatever it took to repair my body. Half of your old day off becomes work. Getting your body right. Making sacrifices to achieve your goals.

The fitness evolution I underwent during my sabbatical was implemented with one express purpose: to win the World Cup. But the work I did then and the new habits I formed had the added bonus of allowing me to play for five years after that. I'd evolved from a player contemplating retirement to one capable of playing into my late thirties – something I didn't ever even dream possible when I was relearning how to lift weights.

As I evolved I also began to understand that a bigger part of my role was about working on how I can get the best out of the players around me, which I didn't really understand as much early on, but which I really came to appreciate later and then put into practice during my time in France. It's a transition anyone on a leadership journey will have to make. The junior art director in an advertising company who one day becomes creative director will move from being focused on their own work and their own role, to taking responsibility for teams of people and learning how to get the best out of them. The same for the office junior who one day becomes CEO, and indeed anyone who moves into a leadership position.

EVOLVING A CULTURE TAKES TIME

Following the 2015 World Cup, I started my three-year contract with Racing 92 in France midway through their Top 14 season, the domestic competition in France. Moving to France was an incredible opportunity for me and my family. The opportunity to experience a new culture, learn a new language, forge some new friendships and indulge in some of the finest food and drink in the world was an opportunity we were really grateful for and privileged to be able to do. And being open to the possibility of growth was essential to this.

Weekly French lessons were obligatory in order to live there. I'd never done any language lessons at school bar six months of Japanese lessons, which at the time made me think, *What on earth am I doing this for? I'm never going to use this.* But as New Zealand is so far from any other country with a different native language, I'd never had to learn French. But I had that growth mindset and I wanted to get better. So I did extra lessons to try to get myself up to speed and improve my communication skills. There were other English speakers in the squad, of course, but the coaches communicated in French and expected us to be able to reach a point where we could keep up.

Now, I'm certainly not suggesting I'll be translating this book into the French-language edition any time soon, but I did finally reach a point in my last six months at Racing where I could hold a normal conversation in French. (Some of my French teammates might feel differently about what I was doing to their language, of course.) It might have taken a while to get there, but it was definite growth. And being open to these opportunities to push yourself, to always be open to learning, filters through everything that you do, building confidence and fulfilment in ways you hadn't considered before. It was in stark contrast to the start of my time there, when it was an incredibly humbling, frustrating and restrictive experience to be on the wrong side of the language barrier. And it wasn't just the language to get up to speed with – there were significant cultural differences within the team environment.

One of my first sessions when I joined Racing was a review of a game. The coaches took the whole session and the players didn't say a word. The players just didn't seem that engaged. My first understanding was that the coaches just coached and the players just played. I came out of the meeting thinking, *That's very different.*

In my experience, both with the All Blacks and the Crusaders, the players are the ones playing so they should be giving feedback and running the meeting. From what I could see here in France, the players were being given a game plan and told just to implement that.

Now, some people might be comfortable with that, but if you want to achieve growth and aspire to excellence, you need to evolve and develop more control on the field. If things change during a match you have to adjust, but that's harder to do if you're used to being told what to do. If you're not a collaborative part of the process, then you're not going to be able to think for yourself properly on the field of play. But if you do this work together, if you're able to experiment and challenge each other, to work out your own answers to tough questions, it's going to be easier to figure solutions out on the pitch.

I felt the players weren't contributing enough and that the coaches should be involving them more. *How can we change this so it's not 'coaches and players', it's 'team'?* I thought. *Let's challenge the coaches and they can challenge us.*

Having said this, we had a fantastic year. We won the Top 14 – the club's first win since 1990, a *twenty-six-year* hiatus I was proud to be involved in ending – and reached the final of the European Champions Cup. And while it was disappointing to lose that final to Saracens and limp off injured during the game, I went away at the end of the season feeling that there was so much potential for growth in this team.

By this stage of my career I'd grown as a leader and learned more about how I could contribute off the field as well as on it. My bittersweet experience in 2011, when I did what I could to help the team and support the number 10s despite the fact that my World Cup was over, and my growing role in the All

Blacks leadership group had been good growth experiences for me.

During the off-season I thought I could bring some of that experience to bear. Creating a leadership group seemed like a good place to start: a group of senior players to work closely with the coaches, to challenge and help them and also to provide a good link, a line of communication, between the players and coaches.

My evolution during my sabbatical started with baby steps, learning to lift weights properly again. And particularly when evolving a team or company culture, it's doubly important not to move too fast in case you lose people along the way. With the All Blacks, I'd been used to having two to three leadership meetings a week. So I thought I'd start this new French leadership group with just one meeting a week. Every Monday we would review the game and the previous week, and look at how best to plan the week ahead from a players' point of view.

I think it's fair to say the leadership group wasn't an unqualified success at first. There was a small part of me that felt some of the players didn't want to be there, that it was taking extra time out of their day. Again, I looked back to a key All Black value: *no individual is bigger than the team.* Was the team coming first? I didn't have that trust initially. Obviously, the players cared; they wanted to win. But were they all open to going that extra mile? To come in on their day off? I questioned that.

It was a challenging time. The coaches weren't used to dealing with the players that way. They liked to show the owners they had control of the team. They were paid to coach, after all, not to hand responsibility over to the players. That would look like the players were doing their job, and the coaches were protective of their role.

There were a few New Zealand players at Racing. The likes of Joe Rokocoko, Chris Masoe, Ben Tameifuna and Casey Laulala, so it wasn't a huge period of adjustment for them. And with some support from them and from others, we were able to make some small, incremental changes. But I eventually reached a point in my second season, when I'd had some injuries and I was in a pretty bad mental space, where I just gave up on the leadership group. I stopped calling the meetings.

It left me thinking that you just can't change a culture. The All Blacks cultural reset in 2004 was less a revolution than it was an evolution of values we already possessed. It came from looking back at where we'd come from, identifying those key values and emphasising them in a manner that was relevant to that new generation of players. What I was trying to help introduce at Racing wasn't something innate in their culture: it was something new. And as slowly as I thought we were bringing it in to the environment, perhaps it was still too fast when trying to change something as rigid as a culture, a hierarchy. Perhaps I should have been more patient.

Sure enough, later in this second season, Juan Imhoff, the Argentine wing and fullback, and Yannick Nyanga, the French flanker, came to me and said, 'Come on, man. We need this leadership group.' The second season hadn't been going well, especially after the highs of the first, and like a lot of things in sport – in any discipline – poor results drove a desire to change. But there were other factors at play, too, including a significant disconnect between the coaches and the players about how we wanted to play the game. Juan and Yannick were brave enough to step forward and say they saw value in the leadership group. They were willing to commit to it.

We pulled together and tried it for a second time, and this time there was some real commitment there. It was incredible, really inspiring. We built some really good relationships with the coaches, and now that we could all see the value in having the group there was some real growth. By my last season the coaches seemed more open-minded about working with the players, about growing the game plan and asking for and receiving feedback. There were a lot more one-to-ones with players, and the whole thing felt more open.

When it came time for me to leave Racing in 2018, I did so feeling that I'd been able to do what was ingrained in us to do as All Blacks: to leave the environment in a better place. To add to the legacy. We had a strong season in the Top 14 and reached the final of the European Champions Cup again, losing a close final to Leinster. But more importantly, even though I'd started well and then plateaued a bit, with some frustration, I felt there were some strong foundations established for the future. I knew Racing weren't going to be near the bottom of their division any time soon, and I felt really proud to have played my part in helping shape that environment and leaving it behind.

Because what I learned is that, in fact, you *can* change a culture. You just can't change a culture *too quickly*. It was just that initial setting up and doing something new, something alien to the prevailing culture, that was uncomfortable. Given a suitable period to evolve, the environment gradually changed and people I'd initially thought weren't interested in being part of it began to accept and contribute. It just needed some time.

ARE YOU ABLE TO EVOLVE?

Part of the All Blacks repurposing in 2004 involved a changing of the guard: the coaches put their faith in youth, some established senior players weren't picked again, and some players who had been discarded from the All Blacks set-up found themselves back in the fold. As teams evolve and grow, the personnel inevitably change: players get older while younger ones come through; tactics and the nature of the game evolves; and coaches come and go, or decide they want to move the team in a new direction.

It's the same in business. As an organisation grows, the personnel will inevitably have to change or adapt, which brings to mind the title of Marshall Goldsmith's book once again – *What Got You Here Won't Get You There*. Leaders in growing businesses are left with plenty of questions as they look to the future. Are the people who have taken you this far the right people to take you to the next level? Some of your people might be experienced at doing their job to a certain scale, but are they capable of doing it at the sort of scale you're aspiring to next? Will you need to bring in new expertise? Is the culture you have now the right one to take you forward, or does it need revisiting and potentially evolving? Are you accelerating cultural evolution too quickly – or too slowly? Are the people you have now the right cultural fit for where your organisation is heading? And how do you maintain excellence under pressure while embracing a growth mindset where mistakes are inevitable – what growth-mindset expert Eduardo Briceño calls 'the performance paradox' in his book of the same title?

It's the organisations that answer these questions best that will be able to grow and evolve – and deliver lasting success.

SOME CULTURAL ASPECTS ARE NOT UP FOR DEBATE

When changing a culture, you have to accept that what worked in one environment isn't necessarily going to work in the next. I don't want this book to come across as suggesting that everyone in the world should be doing as the All Blacks do, as that simply isn't true. It wouldn't work in all cultures.

I'd already spent some time in France, during my first sabbatical playing for Perpignan, where I'd seen a different kind of culture at play, so Racing didn't entirely come as a shock. I knew there were some aspects that you just can't change. Lunch, for example. It's a cliché to say about the French, but lunch is a very serious business over there. France is home to sensational food and drink, and part of the culture over there is to have a couple of hours between trainings in the middle of the day for a good lunch.

Every day, a three-course meal of excellent quality would be laid on for us. For anyone new to come in and decide to change that would be unlikely to last long in the job, because it's part of not only the club culture, but their national culture. You can't change things like that. It isn't like working towards having the coaches and players work more closely together, which is something I identified that could be changed.

Instead, with these aspects that aren't up for debate, you need to come to appreciate their permanence and look at what they bring. You will need to be the one to adapt, rather than the culture itself, and you can then find ways to make them work for you. Through this lens lunch is a daily team-building exercise, and you then learn to do your work around it, to have some of the player-to-player conversations or player-to-coach conversations over lunch instead of grabbing a quick coffee or scheduling in a meeting as I might have done in the All Blacks environment.

There were other cultural aspects that I found different in France, too. The team needed more emotive energy – slapping each other and banging their heads – to fire them up before going into battle. However, before a match in New Zealand, our forwards would just be chilling out with their headphones on. They know they can bring the physicality with a flick of the switch come game time. If they were geeing themselves up like the Perpignan players, we'd think something was wrong – that they were working themselves into a state of red and would probably give a whole load of penalties away at the start of the game. But that was another way in which I learned that different cultural approaches could not be reworked into a 'one size fits all' approach.

I felt that relying on this emotive energy led to inconsistent preparation and results. You can't guarantee you'll be able to replicate that kind of emotional energy week in, week out. This isn't to say that their approach didn't work, of course. You only have to look at how well the France national team had played against the All Blacks at World Cups to see how effective it could be. But the fact remained that, at the time of writing, they hadn't won a World Cup, and that's down to consistency, being able to deliver those world-class performances back to back.

But then, that emotional approach is part of their culture. If you tried to take it away, would it make them more consistent? Or less able to reach the dizzying heights? Is it an immovable part of their culture or one that could be evolved? These questions are challenges of the sort that anyone faces when looking at a culture, and often it comes down to a simple question: does the culture need to evolve here, or do I need to adapt?

CIRCUMSTANCES AND OPPORTUNITIES DRIVE EVOLUTION

A big part of evolution, whether it's on an individual level or a collective one, is the ability to be open to new things – to have a growth mindset. That way, when circumstances and challenges come along, we're able to see them as opportunities, not problems. Similar to how we came to embrace pressure, to walk towards it, so changes in circumstance – some which might be planned, others certainly not so – can be something we walk towards with the knowledge that an opportunity for growth is at hand.

The coaches selecting me as the first-choice number 10 on the November tour in 2004 was one such piece of circumstance that was an incredible opportunity for me. Their decision changed my position in the team, from a 12 to a 10, and allowed me to evolve into the player I became. Similarly, less pleasant circumstances in 2011 that saw me miss the rest of the World Cup, offered me the opportunity to have one more crack at the World Cup and helped cement the team's evolution from great to great.

What I've come to learn is that you can make all the plans you want, but change is often a result of circumstances, sometimes out of your control. And it is how you evolve as a consequence of those circumstances that determines whether you're going to be successful or not.

In my last year at Racing 92, I hurt my knee in a game, and the initial verdict was that I'd done my anterior cruciate ligament (ACL). As a player, when you hear something like that your heart drops. I was thirty-six at the time and you don't come back from that. I went into a dark place, but then later found out it was only a partial tear. Whether that was lost in translation, I'm not sure. I paid my own way to see a specialist in Ireland, where my life followed a strict regimen: wake up, train, eat, recover for ninety minutes. Do it again. Do it again. Back to hotel, pool recovery, ice, eat, sleep. Repeat for five days straight for three weeks.

It was brutal. But it meant I came back, and I felt re-energised and determined to finish the season with a bang.

During my absence I had lost my place in the team, to the South African player Pat Lambie, and I played a lot of rugby off the bench, which I accepted. Putting the team first was good experience to put into practice. I could still contribute with the leadership group, which we had got working really well in that final season, and when I came off the bench I was determined to play out of my skin. I had some great games from the bench, such as the European Champions Cup quarter-final against Clermont. I had evolved into a player able to make an impact in shorter periods later in the game.

Following my final season in France in 2018, I joined Kobe Steelers in Japan, where the irony of wondering at school why on earth I would ever need to learn Japanese wasn't lost on me. During my final year with Kobe in 2020, when the pandemic struck, the season was cancelled and my plans for a grand swansong lay in tatters and I eventually retired, I experienced a huge and sudden change in my life thanks to circumstances well and truly out of my control. And it's how I evolve from this, what my life post rugby will look like, that will ultimately determine whether I'll be successful or not.

But with a growth mindset, being open to new things and embracing a cultural change in my own life, I am confident that I'm standing at the beginning of the second peak of my career – one that will be higher than the first because of all the experience I've acquired along the way.

THREE POINTS – STAYING AHEAD OF THE COMPETITION

1. The Art of Winning could just as easily be called the art of evolution. Consistent success doesn't come from remaining consistent in your attributes; it means expanding your skillset and constantly evolving just to keep at that top line. For teams and organisations, it means ensuring that you have the people and attributes to get you where you want to go – not just those that have got you this far.

2. Evolve a culture gradually, especially if it involves brave new ways, but be mindful that some cultural norms are set in stone. Ask yourself, *Do I need to adapt or does the culture?*

3. Do you have a beginner's mindset? Are you humble enough to go back to basics to achieve your goals? Sometimes you need to take baby steps before you can walk, let alone run.

You can't ape the characteristics of other leaders, even those you admire, if it isn't part of who you are. Develop your own leadership style and make it unique to you.

CHAPTER 9

IDENTITY

At the end of my first season in France, it's fair to say things were going pretty well. On the field, I'd come off the back of a successful season, during which I'd won the World Cup with the All Blacks and the Top 14 in France with Racing. Off the field, there was no end of sponsorship opportunities on the table and living in Paris meant that for the first time in my life, I was enjoying success without anyone really knowing who I was. Parisians didn't really care about seeing a rugby player in a restaurant or walking down the street. It was a new experience, to have some sense of normality back in everyday life.

I might have been getting a little ahead of myself. I might have even started to believe I was a little bit of a rock star. Honor and our two young boys, Marco and Fox, were living with me in Paris, but I might also have been a bit removed from family and friends in New Zealand. I was living in a bit of a bubble.

My second season at Racing wasn't going quite as well as the first had. I struggled with injuries, struggled at times with motivation and drive. I detailed my frustrations with the leadership group in the last chapter, but I was also frustrated with my own performances on the field. In February 2017, midway through the season in France and during the break for the Six Nations we had every year, Honor and the kids flew back to New Zealand. I was due to follow them.

I was driving home through Paris the night before I was due to fly back to New Zealand. I saw a flashing blue light in my rear-view mirror. I pulled over. *Stupid, stupid, stupid.*

My French was still a work in progress, but I quickly gathered I'd been pulled over for driving over the speed limit. Truth be told, I already knew. Then they got the breathalyser out and asked me to blow into it. I already knew what would happen then.

I was over the limit. Of course I was. *How could you be so stupid?*

The police took me off to the station, where I spent the night in a cell. From the high of winning the Top 14 to sitting in a cell in Paris. That's the world bringing you back to earth.

Except it isn't the world. Because there was no one other than myself to blame for an act of such reckless stupidity that it still makes me feel sick talking about it – sick writing it down here.

You idiot.

You could have hurt someone – killed someone.

'No dickheads'?

Is this what an All Black great does?

When I should have been flying home the next day to be with my family, I instead had a very tough phone call to make. Honor was furious with me. She had every right to be. It wasn't just about me anymore: I was the father to two young children. A husband to her. *What was I playing at?*

I don't think the police who arrested me knew who I was when they picked me up originally, but by the time we got back to the station they might have realised there would be some outside interest in the story. I knew the only course of action was to front up and face the consequences.

I lost my Land Rover sponsorship, and quite rightly so. I would have understood if other sponsors had jumped ship too. The media camped outside my house in New Zealand for a week. You don't always think about it at the time that these events are happening, but the effect they have on the people around you, the people who love you, is profound.

The story was in the press, so *everyone* knew about it. Now, that's one thing for me to have to deal with – I'm the one who messed up, after all – but it's quite another for my wife, my parents, my friends to have to deal with the consequences too. It wasn't fair on them.

A setback like this isn't something you build in 'time to grieve'. There's no process for this. It's entirely of my own making, so you have to own up to the mistake straight away and be prepared to face the music. I knew I'd massively messed up, knew it was one of the most stupid things I'd done in my life. I'm not perfect, far from it. Twelve years after jumping in a taxi from Wales to London with my teammates, I was still capable of doing something stupid, despite the wealth of life experience I'd acquired since then. But this was worse, of course. Far worse. I'd been disrespecting the culture and sabotaging my own career then: this could have ended in far more severe consequences, and to this day I'm so grateful I didn't injure anyone on the roads.

Earlier in the book I talked about **better people make better All Blacks** – the 'no dickheads' policy, if you like. For some people, that sounds like you have to be some kind of anointed saint to be in the All Blacks environment, but that isn't what it means at all. 'No dickheads' means you have people in the environment who put the team first. It doesn't mean someone who might make a mistake, be a 'dickhead' on a one-off occasion but be able to own their failings and make amends.

I'd been a dickhead back in 2005 when we took that taxi to London, no question about that. This incident in France went far beyond that, it was pure reckless stupidity. But it was a mistake.

Messing up like this raises questions about who you really are, deep down. What your identity is. Where you've come from. Was I someone who was going to continue down this path? Was this incident completely in character with me as a person? Or was I someone who was going to face up to the consequences and move on?

I don't believe this incident was reflective of who I was as a person. I believe it might have been part of a path I was walking down, but the best thing I could do was remember where I had come from. And flying home to New Zealand to face up to the consequences was essential to remind myself just who I am.

NEVER FORGET WHERE YOU CAME FROM

What are your roots? If Chapter 2, in which we looked at whakapapa and legacy, was about learning where you've come from in order to go forward, then this chapter is about never forgetting where you've come from in order to remain faithful to and authentic as the person you are. It's about knowing your identity, your core values and beliefs, the touchstones which allow you to see if you're remaining true to who you are.

I've talked throughout this book about the importance of being focused on goals and purpose, about striving for greatness, whatever form that may take. But what I came to realise is that it's important to be able to take a break from this as well. To switch off, step back and spend time with loved ones. My family and friends played such a part in providing that and in helping me to have the success that I did.

They're the people I need when things aren't going well but more importantly when they are. They keep me grounded. I've tripped up on many occasions, maybe read my own press at times, started to believe the hype on some level. But my friends, my family and especially my wife have always been there for me. They are key to my identity.

My roots are in Southbridge, of course, a small farming community south-west of Christchurch in the South Island of New Zealand. I'm really proud of where I come from. No matter where I am in the world, I still see myself as being a country boy from Southbridge. And during my playing career I'd go back there whenever I got the chance. It's home for me.

I still have a lot of old friends there, including people I went to school with – friends who have known me my whole life. When I go back, even if I haven't seen some of these friends for a long time – and I definitely don't get to see them as much as I'd like these days – it feels like we always pick things up as if it were just yesterday. These are friends who know me for who I am, not what I've achieved.

Spending time with friends like this and family always gave me a healthy reality check during my playing career. When I was playing a Test match for the All Blacks, I might make nine out of ten kicks, but I guarantee you that the only one my friends will remind me about after the game is the one I missed. They wouldn't let me get too big for my boots.

After doing the rehab for my injury in 2009, when I ruptured my Achilles tendon, I played for Southbridge against Hornby as part of my return to match fitness. It was such a proud moment for me, the first time since I was seventeen that I'd put on the Southbridge jersey. I'd only ever played age-grade rugby for them before. At amateur level, they play with whatever balls they have available, so I brought four beautiful new balls to play the match with. I was kicking that day so I wanted to make sure I knew what I was going to be kicking.

I missed my first five kicks. The crowd of a couple of thousand people couldn't believe what they were seeing. Towards the end of the match, I ran something like fifty metres to score a try. An opposing player was hot on my tail but I was so desperate to get it under the posts and have an easy conversion that when I kicked it between the posts the whole crowd cheered, somewhat ironically, at my one successful kick out of six. That brought me right down to earth.

If I ever reached a point where I felt I'd outgrown Southbridge, where my family and old school friends were no longer as important to me, I know it would be time to give myself a strong talking-to, a slap to the leg to get me focused back on the present, on what's real. Because that's not who I am.

WHO'S ON YOUR SUPPORT SQUAD?

Who do you turn to in times of crisis? Everyone needs a good team around them – whether that's a partner, family or friends, or colleagues. We all need people who aren't afraid to give it to us straight, who are pulling in the same direction as us and crucially people with whom we can switch off away from the pressures of work. These relationships need regular maintenance and can't be neglected – because without them, there's always the danger you can lose sight of who you really are.

In 2020, when I'd played my last game of professional rugby but didn't yet know it, I did something unthinkable. I agreed to play for the Blues, Auckland's Super Rugby team.

Anyone who has followed my career will know that I was a Crusaders man. I'd played for the Canterbury team for the entirety of my career in New Zealand in the Super Rugby competition. My colours, at least where Super Rugby was concerned, were the red and black of the

Crusaders – not the Blues. The Blues were the great rivals. The enemy.

When the Blues player Stephen Perofeta was injured, their coach Leon MacDonald said to me, 'Come back and play.'

'I can't,' I said. 'I'm a Crusader, through and through. I can't play for the Blues.'

But Leon had caught me at a weak moment and I eventually said, 'Yes, I'll come and train.'

Suddenly, I was putting on the Blues training kit, which was something I never thought I'd do. It was one of the weirdest feelings I've ever had. The kit was sitting in the changing room and Jared, the social media manager, was there to record the moment. But I just needed a little moment, to ask myself, *What am I doing?*

As soon as I was out on the rugby pitch with a training ball in my hand, I knew this was what I had been missing. It gave me reassurance. Throughout the pandemic I'd missed rugby. I still wanted to play, to contribute. I had to admit that I was really lucky to be playing a sport I loved while the rest of the world was dealing with Covid.

As fate would have it, I never ended up playing for the Blues. Thanks to injury, I was only available for the final game of the season – against the Crusaders, of course – and Leon had to break it to me over the phone that I wouldn't be playing. We got a Covid community case in Auckland shortly afterwards and we were put into lockdown straight away. The game never happened.

Sometimes when you do things you never imagined you would, the way to remain true to your identity can get lost in all manner of other concerns. Sometimes financial concerns might mean you have to take a role or go somewhere that isn't necessarily aligned with your identity, and you don't have much choice in those circumstances. But in my case the motivation was driven by the fact that I didn't want to retire, I was desperate to remain in the rugby world. And experiences like this often teach you things. One thing my brief time with the Blues crystallised for me was that I had no drive left to play professional rugby in New Zealand. I was finished.

Of course, that still meant I was able to go back and play amateur rugby for Southbridge: a team built into the fabric of my identity. Playing and winning in the final of the Coleman Shield brought my career full circle, back to the beginning, a place I'll never forget I came from.

REAL SELF, NOT IDEAL SELF

Never forgetting where you came from isn't the preserve only of people like me, from a small farming town where a hardworking ethos and respect were ingrained in me. It's a value that can be part of anyone, whether they're from an incredibly privileged background or from a difficult upbringing. It isn't necessarily about the place they've come from as much as it is about who you are. Never forgetting where you came from is about staying true to your key values, who you are deep down. People change, of course, but it's about remaining true to those core values, the things about yourself that you can't change that we explored in Chapter 2.

In the All Blacks environment we used to talk about how necessary it was to bring your *real self, not ideal self*. And what that meant was that a lot of people would come into the environment feeling they had to act in a certain way, to behave in a way that wasn't true to who they are as individuals.

It can be quite challenging coming into an environment like that for the first time. You've suddenly got cameras following you everywhere, you have to do media interviews, there's free stuff being sent your way. It's a definite period of adjustment. But what's important throughout this is to be true to the person you are. There is no 'ideal' version of you – only you. There's a double-page spread in the All Blacks book in which Gilbert Enoka contrasts the 'fictional self' with the 'real self', which demonstrates just how important this value is in the environment.

Of course, this type of 'real self' identity can be just as easily applied to teams and organisations. Working out the core values of your team or organisation, just as we did in Chapter 2, can be crucial in helping it re-establish its real self when you've lost your way.

My friend Rob Fyfe is the former CEO of Air New Zealand, who turned the fortunes of the ailing airline around between 2005 and 2012. When he took over the company in 2005 he describes it as a 'faded beauty', which had suffered from underinvestment, and he restored the airline to its place as one of the best in the world. His mission, he says, was to 'rekindle New Zealanders' love affair with their national airline'. The way in which he did this was to remind the business where it came from, and to reconnect with his own and the airline's 'Kiwi-ness', as he puts it. 'It wasn't about planes, it's a business about people,' he says, and through reminding itself where it came from, re-establishing the airline's core identity – its real self – and connecting with its users, Air New Zealand flourished on his watch.

BEING YOUR REAL SELF AS A LEADER

Every leader has his or her own individual style. Our amazing coaching trio of Graham Henry, Wayne Smith and Steve Hansen were incredibly different yet complementary characters.

Wayne Smith was the professor, a workaholic who spent so much time analysing the opposition, analysing his own players and challenging them. He can be direct and intense, and gets frustrated when he feels people aren't giving it their all.

Steve Hansen was the coach that you could go and have a beer with; he was more relaxed, a different character from Wayne Smith. But he seemed to have this intuitive understanding of the game that I'd never seen before – he seemed to be able to see something and pinpoint exactly what needed to be done about it.

And then you had Graham Henry, the former head-master who was the perfect person to be in charge. He would oversee everything – he'd seen it all – and wouldn't feel the need to say an awful lot unless it was important. But when he did speak, you listened. His famous dry sense of humour in interviews actually belied quite a caring, inclusive side to him: he was always the first one to go over and say hello to the families and make them feel included.

These are just three examples of very different charac-ters who are successful leaders, and the key for you as a leader is to be your real self. You can't ape the char-acteristics of other leaders, even those you admire, if it isn't part of who you are. Develop your own leadership style and make it unique to you, because people will quickly see through you if you're faking it.

A useful exercise would be to ask yourself, 'Which three words would I use to describe my strengths as a leader?' Do these words align with your core values? Do you think these words would be how your team or other leaders perceive you – or is there a disconnec-tion between the ideal self you're portraying and the real self you imagine you're being?

GRATITUDE

In 2007, when we were preparing for the World Cup later that year, the All Blacks coaches decided to take a few of us out of the first half of the Super Rugby season to train and condition us. The idea was that they didn't want us to play too much rugby and overload ourselves before the World Cup.

During this time I learned how much trouble Southbridge rugby club were in. One of the most historic grassroots rugby clubs in New Zealand, they were now in danger of dropping down to the second division and were struggling even to put a team together each week. A lot of country sides face this problem. As kids finish high school and move on to the big city, it makes it hard to find the numbers.

As I wasn't playing at the weekend I had some extra time on my hands, so I decided to go and do some coaching at Southbridge. Some good mates of mine were still playing for the club, and coming home felt good. I decided to become one of the sponsors of the club that I had played with until the age of seventeen. I really felt I needed to give back to the club that had given me so much. The club had a couple of tough years after that, but things got a lot better afterwards. We've got some really good numbers now and some really good players, and I've been affiliated with Southbridge ever since.

To this day I feel grateful to the club, for it being the scene of so many amazing memories from my youth. It's the place of so many memories from my dad's own youth too: he's been part of Southbridge for so long. It's such a big part of the Carter family history.

This sense of gratitude in lots of things in my life and career is one that became more prevalent and important as I got older. I felt grateful to have come from where I did: where a strong work ethic was instilled in a loving home from my parents, a home in which my rugby-mad dad always encouraged but never pushed me towards the game.

Matthew Syed is a British journalist and bestselling author specialising in high performance. He is also the former number one British table tennis player, and in his book *Bounce* he describes the 'powerful advantages not available to hundreds of thousands of other youngsters' he had as a child that helped his ascent to become the player he was: he was given 'a full size, tournament-specification table' at the age of eight; he had an older brother who was an excellent table tennis player and with whom he was 'blissfully accumulating thousands of hours of practice'; the top table tennis coach in the country taught at the local primary school; and his local table tennis club was open twenty-four hours a day and included some of the top young players in the country among its members.

Reading this, I couldn't help but think about my own youth and the powerful advantages I enjoyed. I grew up in pretty much the perfect rugby-nurturing environment: Dad was an experienced player and coach whose life was based around rugby; I was given full-size rugby posts in our garden for my eighth birthday (which must be even more uncommon than having a full-size table tennis table in a large garage); I had a rugby club a few minutes' walk from our house; and I accumulated thousands of hours of practice as a result. And that's before I consider the genetic advantages that gave me a low centre of gravity, good feet and hand-eye co-ordination.

It's a powerful exercise to consider these advantages, to become aware of them and be grateful for them. Of course, these aren't the only reasons I became the player I was – there was a whole load of work to do, which I've detailed through-out this book. But the point is that my obligation is no different from yours: to make the most of what we're given. We aren't all made the same, but even the gifted can't be great without the graft.

> **WHAT ARE YOUR ADVANTAGES?**
>
> Are you able to identify them and be grateful for them? How have they helped you to get to where you are in life? And are you maximising them to unlock your true potential?

My second season at Racing hadn't gone well: the injuries, my frustration with my form and the leadership group, the team fail-ing to back up the success we'd enjoyed the previous year, the drink-driving charge. These weren't things I was going to look back on fondly.

But when we came back for my third and final season in France, with a proper pre-season, it was with a renewed sense of purpose. I'd had time to put things into perspective, and accepted that I was now in the final years of my career and it was about gratitude for me now. I was so lucky to be able to play for so long, and I was incredibly grateful for that. During this third season I felt more settled and part of the environ-ment, we got the leadership group going and I felt so much more motivated. After a difficult season both personally and as a team, it was fantastic to enjoy some success in that final season, impacted though it was by my ACL injury midway through.

By the time I made it to Japan to be reunited with Wayne Smith at Kobe Steelers in 2018, gratitude became an even bigger part of my identity. *You're not going to last ten more years,* I said to myself. *These are the last ones. Enjoy playing in a team environment. Be grateful for every last minute you're out on the field. You're going to finish your career on your terms – on a high.*

Some days I might get out of bed and not feel much like training, but then I'd say to myself, *This is going to be one of your last trainings. One of the last seasons you can call yourself a rugby player.* I felt incredibly grateful for the opportunity, in what I felt sure was to be my last ever professional contract.

It was a feeling that was amplified by my recovery from the ACL injury that derailed my last season in France. At the time, I thought that was it. My career was over. But like so many other setbacks before, I'd managed to come back from it, and every day I spent playing felt like a gift. Or at least it did most of the time. I'm only human, after all. Some days I had to remind myself to be grateful, but what I discovered is that gratitude is like so many other habits: it can be developed over time.

Wayne Smith said to me at Kobe, 'You already plan your week, why don't you take the time to just add a few things you're grateful for. You're so regimented that you might skip gratitude, but it's important.' He encouraged all the players to do it.

So now I have my gratitude book. I try to write three things in it every day before I go to sleep that I'm grateful for. Don't get me wrong, I repeat myself – a lot. But I find it really useful, especially after a tough day, to be able to write down the things I'm grateful for, such as having my health, my family, being able to eat nutritious food every day.

These are things many of us take for granted, but they help me overcome that voice in my head that pipes up from time to time, complaining about things. They help me put things in perspective, see that things could be so much worse. Just as when looking at whakapapa and our personal and collective purpose, gratitude provides a connection with something bigger than myself, bigger even than with my immediate family. I find it incredibly powerful.

Consistency is the biggest challenge a lot of us face when trying to change any habit, and that's why writing it down every day is so important. For some people that might mean writing it on a phone or tablet, or even using a voice memo, but for me it's always been about physically writing it in a book. Like I have said before, you need to find ways to make habits become second nature, which is why I find physically writing everything down – goals, gratitude, weekly plans – really connects me to it and commits me to doing it.

That constant, habit-based approach eventually pays off, because by regularly reminding yourself of what you have to be grateful for you become more aware of it generally. It helps put things into perspective. It's a really important tool to keep your feet on the ground, to never let you get ahead of yourself. And it also has a positive impact on mental health. Making gratitude a habit trains the brain – repurposes it, if you like – to tune in to the more positive things in life, to seek out more reasons for gratitude.

It's a practice that has certainly helped me later in my career and during this period of repurposing in my life. The work I've done with UNICEF has helped open my eyes to the fact that so many children are living in poverty. Many children in the Pacific Islands don't have access to clean water, sanitation and hygiene facilities, things I've taken for granted in my own life.

Many of us have reason to be so incredibly grateful for things we might not always appreciate. Being grateful for what you have was put to the test during the Covid pandemic. When faced with the reality that I wouldn't be finishing my career on my terms, that I was effectively going to be forced into retirement, I found it an incredibly challenging and difficult time. But at the same time, what I was going through was nothing compared to the real heartache and suffering going on around the world.

Sometimes it's difficult to get that kind of perspective. I certainly found it a challenge at the time. And that's because you can still be grateful for your circumstances and be disappointed when things go wrong for you personally. I felt for anyone suffering from that terrible virus and its consequences, the bigger picture, and at the same time felt genuine disappointment and confusion about my career. These aren't two mutually exclusive things.

But what remained during those times was my feeling of gratitude: of knowing that I had a healthy family in a country that was able to protect itself from the worst of the pandemic at that time. The way my career finished was disappointing, of course, but learning to be grateful for what I had, rather than focusing on what I did not, certainly allowed me to be able to process that disappointment with a better sense of perspective.

TAKE A LEAF OUT OF WAYNE SMITH'S BOOK

Why not give a gratitude journal a try? It needn't be a huge commitment – just writing down three things you're grateful for on a piece of paper or on your phone at the end of each day. It's OK to repeat yourself, and if you can turn it into a habit it's a good way to finish the day on a positive note and to develop a more attuned sense of gratitude for the things you do have – and not worry about those that you don't.

THREE POINTS - IDENTITY

1. When you mess up you need to 'fess up: is this a true reflection of who you are? Face the consequences, learn from your mistake and move on.

2. Real self, not ideal self: only authenticity will do in an environment where everyone is aspiring to be the best they possibly can. Just be yourself.

3. Make gratitude a habit and it will stop feeling like an abstract concept and start making you grateful for the things you have.

When no one's around to hold you accountable, are you still exploring your limits to improve and get better every time?

CHAPTER 10

SACRIFICE

DO WHAT'S RIGHT WHEN NO ONE'S LOOKING

The Kobe Steelers hadn't won the Japanese Top League since the inaugural tournament in 2003–4. Signing for them in 2018 was the opportunity to earn the respect of a new set of players, fans and coaches; the incredible opportunity to work with their head coach Wayne Smith again; and the chance to experience a new culture. But mainly it was an opportunity to continue playing – to continue *winning*.

I knew this was likely to be my last contract, so I wanted to put everything into it. *Don't think about life after rugby,* I said to myself, *think about being the best player you can for the team, drive the leadership group, drive the standards, drive the culture, but finish on your terms playing at a level that you can be extremely proud of.* That was what was driving me each day. I was trying to avoid thinking about retirement. I was threatened by the very idea of it – even though it was just around the corner.

The Japanese season was amazing. It was a hugely exciting, motivating time, and it brought real focus to my game. I was playing free-flowing rugby, I had my running game back, and I felt really in control. I had a new lease of life and finished the season on a high, not only winning the Top League with the team but collecting an individual accolade as Japanese Top League Most Valuable Player.

At the end of that first season, I had a ten-month break lined up, as the 2019 Rugby World Cup was being hosted by Japan and the new season wouldn't start until after the tournament was over. During the break, my prospective return to Racing as an injury replacement for Pat Lambie was ruled out because of my neck, and I had surgery and rehabbed once again. It was my last major rehab, and yet again required returning to the well of mental strength I'd built up throughout my career.

With a break and no rugby for the next ten months, I had the luxury of a sneak preview of what life was going to be like in retirement. What was I going to miss? In fact, the most pro-found realisation was not about missing rugby but how much I needed my family, and how much they needed me around. It was quite an eye-opener and made me think I'd been selfish in some ways – hiding from retirement, being away from my loved ones. My family didn't care if I was a professional rugby player or not. They just wanted me around.

After the World Cup, I returned to Kobe to start my last ever pre-season. On my first day back, I walked into my apartment and it hit me very clearly: *I shouldn't be here – I should be at home in New Zealand.* And then I was hit by an even stronger sense: *What the hell are you doing?*

My family had sacrificed so much for me. *What are you playing for? Why are you hiding from this life post rugby? What are you so threatened by? What are you trying to prove? Who are you trying to prove it to?*

Luckily, Wayne Smith was there, my old mentor and coach, and we sat down and talked. 'I don't feel like I belong here,' I told him.

He was extremely supportive. 'What do you want to do?' he asked. 'Do you want to go home?'

'No,' I said. And it was true – I didn't. I had a contract that I was going to honour. But I did need to share how I was feeling, just as I had with Gilbert Enoka back in 2005 when I first knocked on his door. I'd grown into a person more comfortable sharing these things, more used to being open and honest about my feelings. *Real self, not ideal self.* I knew I could turn it around and show myself to be the player I'd been the previous season for the team.

It crystallised for me the fact that this was *definitely* my last season. I had sacrificed enough, my family too, by extending my playing career in Japan while they lived in New Zealand. There wasn't going to be another contract, no matter what was on the table. And while Honor said she'd believe it when she saw it, I felt a real sense of control knowing that I was going to finish on my terms. Rugby had given me such a good life, and I was determined to show some gratitude for it. I was convinced it was going to be an even better year than the last one.

ME, ME, ME: WHY YOUR PURPOSE NEEDS TO BE SELF-CENTRED

I have a confession to make: I'm selfish. I'm a dedicated family man who hasn't always put his family first in the pursuit of professional excellence. I'm someone for whom no one is bigger than the team and yet I'm capable of being a selfish individual, putting myself first when I need to. These are contradictions I've had to learn to accept, and if you want to reach the top there's a part of you that simply must do likewise.

Having children changes everything, and you soon learn that it's very challenging to be both a world-class performer and a world-class parent. In fact, I'd go as far as to say I found it impossible to get that balance right. No matter what you do, there will always be sacrifices to be made, and you're going to need a supportive and understanding partner. But I did find that the culture you are a part of can play a big role in helping with that.

I described in Chapter 3 the efforts made in the All Blacks to bring family and work closer together and support the players on an individual basis, so this was a good 'working environment', if you like, for us to have our first child, Marco, in 2013, and then Fox in 2015, just a few months before the World Cup. But there were still sacrifices to be made: after all, I was working towards the World Cup in 2015, the singular focus that had been driving me for four years.

When we lived in New Zealand I was away from home 50 per cent of the time, whether that was games for the Crusaders early in the year or tours with the All Blacks later in the year. This was less of a problem earlier in my career, and Honor was a successful sportsperson and had a successful career in her own right, playing for the Black Sticks – New Zealand's national hockey team – and working in marketing. But once we had children she retired from hockey and gave up her job so we could move to France together.

In France, it was more like 'normal' life – if such a thing exists – in that I was at home a lot more. The most I was away was one night, which allowed me to achieve a better sense of the elusive work–life balance. As Honor is from a sports background, she understands the importance of rest and preparation before the big game. She would be the one getting up to the children in the night.

When I started playing in Japan in 2018, however, Honor and the kids moved back to New Zealand; I would live in Japan for the season, which was six months long. We went back to my being away for 50 per cent of the time, chasing my goals, while Honor looked after the kids. Our third son, Rocco, arrived in early 2019.

I missed my family like crazy when I was away. I hadn't felt guilty about needing the night in a hotel before a game in France – it was necessary and Honor understood – but I now felt guilty about being so far from home for so long while she had our three children. But in order to be successful and play to the best of my abilities, I had to find ways to focus on me – on recovery, preparation. And I found that the key to this was through my personal purpose.

I've known players who, when they have their first child,

change their purpose to be more family-oriented, perhaps to be more about setting themselves up financially and providing for their loved ones. Of course, these are noble intentions that were definitely in my thoughts in just about everything I did in my career. But this simply wouldn't work as a personal purpose for me. To me, these are things that come with the territory of striving towards your purpose – but they can't be the purpose itself.

If you're striving for greatness, exploring the limits of what you're capable of, then a strong personal purpose has to be about yourself (while at the same time be about something bigger than yourself and marry with the *collective* purpose of the team). *To strive to be an All Black great. To get better every day. To leave the jersey in a better place.* It has to be something that provokes an innate, personal reaction, something that resonates deep down in your core. And at the same time it has to operate on a higher plane, be something bigger than the next game, the next goal or even the next year. It connects you directly to this higher calling. It's something you strive towards, not something you ever necessarily achieve.

If your personal purpose or your goals become about your family or financial matters, then it's going to affect the decisions you make for your career: do you choose the option that's going to push and challenge you more, or the better-paid option? The option that allows you to spend more time with your family or the one that offers potential greatness?

There are no right or wrong answers to these questions. Each of us is different, facing different challenges and priorities at different stages of our lives. For many of us, the financial imperatives simply must be met. While lots of us are happy to reach a good balance of career achievement and family life. Even in these scenarios, however, there are still sacrifices to be made. We'll all have times when the balance isn't quite there, when we're working more than usual, perhaps, not finding enough time for the family. Or where we have the family time but work perhaps isn't challenging us enough.

But if you're serious about pushing yourself and achieving big goals, then there is definitely going to be some sacrifice. You're going to need that personal purpose to provoke a strong, innate reaction that drives you on, even when you miss your family and friends like crazy, when it would be tempting to just jack it all in and settle into an easier life.

It was my strong personal purpose, my mental drive that allowed me to drag my battered body first to France and then to Japan, to carry on playing and contributing to the game. To continue to strive to get that little bit better every day. Your body follows your mind through these times, and it was my mental strength that allowed me to do this.

It was this sense of purpose and mental drive that spurred me on during my second season in Japan, even as the call of my family and home grew ever stronger, despite knowing that home was where I *should* be. My purpose allowed me to focus on me, to block out the call of home when I needed to. I felt guilty as hell about it afterwards, but I needed it to drive me.

And my purpose was what allowed me to come back from my personal disappointment in 2011 and play my part off the field in helping the team, and to come back and do it on the field four years later. Because it's this mental reserve, the acceptance that there will be sacrifices along the way, that allows a select number of people to go from good to great – and it's what drives an even more select group who are able to go from great to great.

THE ART OF SUBTRACTION

In the legendary Manchester United manager Sir Alex Ferguson's book *Leading*, I came across a passage that was all too familiar to me – and will be to anyone who has performed at the highest level:

> I have yet to encounter anyone who has achieved massive success without closing themselves off from the demands of others or forgoing pastimes . . . I just cannot imagine how, if you aspire to be better than everyone else, you can have balance in your life.

Ferguson writes about the importance of being able to filter out all the distractions so that you can use your time to focus on your main purpose, and explains that the most successful players who enjoy the greatest longevity are those who can do this most effectively. It's a challenge that is easier when you're a young player, of course, when you have fewer obligations and commitments, and it's an idea that was thrown into sharp focus for me when I retired from rugby.

After retiring, I had a lot of offers and opportunities come my way. And given that retirement was something I'd been dreading for years and I felt lost and completely unsure about what my place in society was – other than 'ex-rugby player' – I found myself saying yes to all of it, because I had no idea what was next, when this might all dry up.

So I found myself taking on sponsorship opportunities, getting involved in three start-ups, designing a pair of rugby boots, doing a book (not this one – this came *after*). And don't get me wrong, I'm really pleased to have done a lot of these things, but I was clearly taking on too much.

What I've discovered is that walking towards a purpose involves no small amount of the art of subtraction. It means saying no to things in your life that are going to potentially get in the way of achieving your main goals. In my case, after retirement it meant taking on fewer but more targeted opportunities. It meant saying no to some opportunities so that I could spend time focusing on repurposing my life. In your own life, it might mean less socialising so you can focus on your purpose or saying no to watching a box set so you can spend that time doing an evening course. For a self-employed person it might mean saying yes to fewer but more fulfilling or better-paid opportunities.

And if we broaden that out beyond the individual it might mean your business doing more to master its core product, rather than being a 'jack of all trades', in order to deliver stronger growth. It might mean spending less time working on the 'weaknesses' in your team and more dedicated to building on its strengths. It could mean fewer meetings involving the whole team and more targeted and efficient one-to-ones or smaller meetings involving the key stakeholders. It could even mean looking at your hybrid-working model and asking if you've got that balance right – do you need to subtract some of that home-working time to get people face to face, collaborating and generating ideas? Or vice versa: do you need to have people spending more time out of the office for focused work with fewer distractions?

Because while the art of subtraction might sound like an inherently negative thing – saying 'no' more often – it's actually a positive approach. What you're actually saying is 'yes' more frequently to your core purpose, the thing that is going to deliver you the most satisfaction and success. Yes, there is going to be sacrifice along the way – you'll say no to some good-looking opportunities as you go, there will be less time with friends and family – but if you're striving towards a suitable purpose, trust me, it won't always feel like sacrifice. It will feel like you're doing the most natural thing in the world – what you were born to do. Just as we did back in Chapter 4 (Mind Management), it will allow you to root yourself in the present and ask, *What's important right now?*

MIND GAMES

Towards the end of my time in France, I started to suffer from a complete and utter lack of energy. Nothing had changed in my diet and the doctors couldn't get to the bottom of it, so I contacted a nutritionist I trusted in New Zealand, Kaytee Boyd, who suggested I do some tests and give blood to analyse my gut health.

The results came back saying that the lining of my stomach was in a bad way. There wasn't much of it left, in fact. I was eating food and it was pretty much just going straight through me, without my body absorbing any of the nutrients. A career spent taking antibiotics, anti-inflammatories and painkillers in order to play, one of the less glamorous but incredibly common aspects of being in professional sports, had wreaked havoc on my gut health, and the prescription from Kaytee to cure it was three months on a strict diet of starchy foods and a lot of vegetables (red cabbage in particular sticks in my memory). I did the work and after the three months were up, my energy levels were back to normal.

At the end of my career, Kaytee asked me, 'Have you ever thought about fasting?' It obviously wasn't an option when I was playing, as I needed to take on plenty of food and energy, but now she introduced a 'fasting mimicking' diet to me, which was basically five days of consuming only 800 calories a day. Honor isn't the biggest fan of me doing this, not least because it means I'm probably going to be weaker, grumpier and not much use with the kids. 'Why don't you just eat healthy all of the time instead?' she asks.

But I still do them once or twice a year. And the answer is partly because of how they make me feel: the first time I did it, once I did my refeed (you don't start eating bad food afterwards – it's always healthy food), it was the best I'd felt in twenty years. I went to the gym and worked out with the Glory Days – the group of ex-players I exercise with when I get the chance – a session that usually wipes me out. This time, though, after the session I decided to go and do some hill repeats – running up a hill ten times. I felt fantastic – and the mental clarity it brings is incredible. It's an amazing way to reset.

What I really like about these fasts is the mental challenge they present: the mind games. I know that at any point during a fast, I can just go into the kitchen and get myself something proper to eat. *Go on, do it,* my mind is saying. *No one is going to know.* It's almost like I've got another person in my head, challenging me. It would be so easy to give in. And yet . . .

I don't give in. And it's this discipline of overpowering my mind, exploring the limits of what I can and can't do that I love. I relish the challenge. It's the willpower that comes from being able to do what's right when no one's looking – and it's a key facet when you're challenging yourself in any discipline, whether you're pushing yourself in the gym or to do better in your job. When no one's around to hold you accountable, are you still exploring your limits to improve and get better every time?

Not everyone has this level of willpower, but if you want real, meaningful success, you need to develop it. Because when it pays off, the rewards far outweigh anything that is just handed to you or falls onto your plate. You've earned it through your own resolve rather than fluking it. I want to work for it, I need to work for it. A lot of people think I've had a lot of opportunities just fall into my lap, that I've been lucky. And yes, you can get lucky and don't think for a moment I don't believe I've had my fair share of it. But you don't get consistently lucky throughout a career. Nobody does. That's when the old quote 'the harder I work, the luckier I seem to get' comes into play. There's a whole lot of stuff that's gone on behind the scenes, pure hard work and grind *when no one's looking*, to be able to live the life that I'm living now.

When I would do a kicking session, I would know how many kicks I needed to do to walk away satisfied. No one would know if I was ten kicks short. But I would. On a Friday afternoon in the middle of summer, the mercury's topping 35 degrees. That voice in my mind pipes up: *What are you kicking for? Go home. Go grab an ice-cold beer and kick back – it's the weekend.*

No way. I like to earn my beer, and the challenge is to stay out there until the work is done. The battle is with no one other than my own mind, but it's one I believe you have to consistently win if you're going to achieve great things. I think that most successful people thrive on these challenges; I know the teammates who finished playing for the All Blacks with me all shared this attitude: they all did what was right when no one was looking. At this level, the biggest competition is with yourself.

CAN YOU WIN YOUR MIND GAMES?

I always prided myself on the work I did behind closed doors – doing what's right when no one's looking. I firmly believe that this kind of mental strength can be worked on and developed, starting with seemingly minor things, so that it becomes a habit. You can ultimately derive more satisfaction from winning these challenges than giving in to temptation. So why not start with a simple mental challenge for yourself – to do what's right when no one's looking? If you're in the gym, it's a sunny day outside and your friends are waiting for you in the park, no one's going to know if you don't finish your workout. Only you. But can you challenge yourself to make sure you finish it properly? If you're at work and tempted to go home before finishing your to-do list, can you win that mental battle and do it to the best of your ability and go home a bit later? Start with something small – it might be as simple as making sure you go for your regular run as normal even though it's cold and wet outside, or forcing yourself to get up instead of hitting snooze in the mornings – and see if you can build it into a habit, so that you eventually start turning the tide against that voice in your head piping up and trying to stop you doing the things that, deep down, you know will be better for your aspirations in the long run.

THE WORK ALWAYS PAYS OFF – JUST NOT ALWAYS STRAIGHT AWAY

When I was rebuilding my body in 2014, I was a prime example of doing what's right when no one's looking. I was doing back-to-basics exercises, usually alone, and the opportunity for taking the easy way out was always there. That voice inside my head was constantly piping up: *Who's going to know if you take a couple of shortcuts today?*

It was a constant battle with that voice, but I knew that I had to focus on the process, concentrate on that next repetitive action, *be present* and the outcome would take care of itself.

And I knew from experience that if I put in the work, it would pay off in the end.

What I wasn't prepared for, however, was breaking my leg within two months of returning from my sabbatical. I'd eased my way back into playing, first for Southbridge and then the Crusaders, before I went down injured in the Super Rugby final. *Not again,* I thought when I learned the injury was serious. All that work to repair my body and here we were again, back to feeling like I did during the injury-ravaged year of 2013.

My sabbatical probably wasn't ideally timed in terms of aiming for the World Cup in 2015. Taking it the year before the tournament didn't give me a huge amount of time to play my way back into contention. In an ideal world I'd have taken my sabbatical in 2013, but Richie McCaw was taking his own sabbatical then and I had to soldier through the worst season of my career, desperate to get to the end of it. Probably not the most exemplary outlook from a 2012 World Rugby Player of the Year.

This injury so soon after my comeback only served to shrink the already small window in which I could earn my place on the plane to the World Cup. But bizarrely there was a positive I could draw from it: this was a contact injury. Rugby is a contact sport and these injuries can happen at any time, to anyone. This wasn't my body breaking down as it had during 2013. This was different. For some reason this offered me hope.

And I was going to need plenty of hope, because it took me a long time to come back from this injury. Some nerve damage delayed my return; I fell once again into the dark place I'd been in mentally during 2013, when I felt my body was failing me. I explained earlier in this book about my road back to fitness for the 2015 World Cup, about how, when I first returned to playing, it was just about survival: hanging on in there. Trying to get through sixty minutes, then eventually eighty – no thought about actually playing well. Until, at last, I had the confidence to do so, to finish the Super Rugby season strongly and have the tournament of my life at the World Cup. But it was some twelve months after putting my body back together that I actually started feeling good again.

Because what I learned is that, if you challenge yourself and do what's right when no one's looking, the work *always* pays off – it just might not pay off straight away. It was a big lesson to absorb late in my career. Early in my career, I did the work and had instant success. I wouldn't say it was easy, but I saw instant results from what I was doing. It would have been easy for me to quit during this 2013–14 period. I'd already achieved a lot in my career, and it would have been so easy to just call time on it. That little voice was piping up the whole time, of course: *What are you punishing yourself for? You're a hundred-cap All Black, a World Cup winner already – why don't you give yourself a break?*

Battling with that voice is a challenge I relish. I sometimes wonder what sort of person I'd be now if I'd listened to those thoughts. If I'd just given up. I hate to imagine. If I'd failed to make the team for the World Cup, or if I'd broken down and been injured, that would have been different. I'd have had to learn to accept that. But if I'd just quit?

I'd be kicking myself to this day. Because I understood the power of doing right when no one's looking. I had faith that the work would pay off eventually. And if you're able to commit to beating your mind at its own games, then you're going to give yourself a chance to be able to achieve great things. And as I discovered at the World Cup, a chance is all you need.

YOU HAVE TO CELEBRATE SUCCESS TOGETHER (BEFORE YOU GO AGAIN)

After the 2015 World Cup final in Twickenham, we're out on the pitch celebrating, and I'm taking it all in with these teammates that I've played with for the last time in the black jersey. We celebrate in the changing room, the culmination of four years' work for the team, the end of a journey that started in the changing room at Eden Park, when I felt so thrilled for the team winning the 2011 World Cup and yet still held on to a thought that wouldn't leave me alone: *This is going to be me in four years' time.*

We've done it. But it doesn't really sink in at first. It's chaos and euphoria and some moments of nostalgia for those of us who have worn the jersey for the last time. **Leave the jersey in a better place.** It's only when we get back to the hotel that it hits me at last. The importance of what we've managed to achieve.

I know what I need: I need to be by myself. I lie down on my bed in my hotel and just stay there for hours, soaking it all in. I know there will be celebrations and ceremonies and parades to come when we return home to New Zealand, having won the World Cup on foreign soil for the first time. I know there'll be more celebrations to come with my teammates and the staff. But for now, I just want to be in this moment, savouring it, being present with it.

I'm a firm believer that in life you need to pause and take these moments in. Yes, you do the work. You push yourself mentally and physically. You challenge yourself to get better every day. But when you work so hard for something and you achieve it, you need to celebrate that. The one thing I didn't need to do on the Monday after winning the World Cup was to sit down and plan my next season, set my goals and what I wanted to try to achieve. You actually need to celebrate – and then you need some time to decompress.

When you've planned your year ahead, whether it's sport or business, you will have certain targets within that year, and if you hit those targets they need to be celebrated. We're very fortunate in rugby in that we have a target just about every week. We have an outcome every match, successful or not, and when it's successful it's important to celebrate it. The chances are you have another target next week, so obviously you can't celebrate it too hard, but it's important that you acknowledge it before you move on to what's next. With business, success can be much more of a slow burn (even in fast-paced start-ups, compared to sport), taking months or even years, though the businesspeople I've spoken with have all said that when you do eventually have success in business it can be incredible, because so much time, work and effort has gone into it.

What is absolutely crucial in any environment, however, be it sport or business, is that you all celebrate success *together*. My favourite time of the week as a player was in the dressing room after the game on a Saturday. That's when we know if we've had success or not. And no matter what the result, in every team I've ever played for there would be a moment when, after the players have showered, everything would stop and we would all sit around in a circle in the dressing room. No matter what anyone is doing, it all stops. This is one of the most sacred moments of the week, when it is just the team: no friends or family, no sponsors or anyone else from outside the environment. And when I say the team, I mean everyone: the whole squad of players, including the backbone; the coaches; the physios, dietitians, doctors, the kit man – *everyone*. We're all on this journey together.

This is when the captain would speak, and he would often talk about the backbone, thanking them for what they've done that week to make our success possible. Then the coaches would speak, and often they'd celebrate something the support staff had done – the phenomenal work the physios did that week, or the kit man. Something we as players, so focused on the game, might not have been aware of. It's just a reminder once again that everyone is giving their absolute best in this environment, everyone is working towards our collective purpose – and it's also a celebration. We're all part of this, and we celebrate together.

DO YOU CELEBRATE TOGETHER?

Do you ensure that your support staff are valued and share in your success? No matter who the star players are in an organisation, nobody does it alone. If you want everyone pulling together and striving towards your collective purpose, then you simply have to share in your successes together, as a collective. Yes, it's the players who garner the public accolades and glory in rugby, but within our environment, we celebrate everyone who allows us to be in a position to go for that glory in the first place. All of our staff knew that they were part of our collective purpose to be the most dominant team in the history of world rugby, and they were willing to deliver the standards in each of their fields necessary to make that happen. You can't expect people to strive towards the collective purpose if they're not made to feel that they're a *vital* part of the team – and celebrating collective success *together* is such an easy and effective way to help make this happen.

GIVE YOUR MOTIVATION TIME TO GROW

With the really big campaigns – for the All Blacks it was the Tri Nations, the Bledisloe Cup and of course the World Cup – you celebrate together at the right time, directly after the event, and then there needs to be a little bit of time before you really get your hands dirty with what's next. For us that could mean weeks or even a month at the end of the season. In a typical year, we'd be playing or training for roughly eleven months. We'd often finish after the series in November, and I'd always use December as a month to decompress and take my mind off rugby. I'd do a bit of training, but nothing like as intense as during the season.

And naturally in that time, I always had days when I'd start to have a new sense of excitement about the following year, or a new source of motivation, or new ideas about how I wanted to grow my game. And it wasn't until January hit that I would think, *Right, I need to get the pen and paper.* All the things that I'd spent December thinking about, reviewing and learning from – things I could do better compared to the previous season – I would commit to paper, and start planning for the year ahead.

After the 2015 World Cup final I knew I needed a month off at home to unwind before starting at Racing; I'd put so much energy into the World Cup that I wouldn't have been able to do myself justice starting with a new club. Then, over the course of that month off, I started feeling my motivation grow at the thought of new challenges, what I wanted to achieve in France. And I think that time off to decompress, re-evaluate my goals and build some new motivation was why I was playing some of my best rugby six or seven months later.

When you have that mindset of going from great to great, you find that during this time off to recharge the batteries, the motivation, the inspiration, the desire to start setting new goals naturally comes back to you much faster. Over your summer holidays, within ten days you have the thought, *Man, I want to get back. I want to get on and set these goals and get started, because next year is going to be even bigger than this year.*

It's a beautiful thing, to naturally be drawn back to what's next, and that comes from the desire to follow success with success, to go from great to great. But it can also be a time to hold yourself back a bit. Because you know that if you go back to work a couple of weeks early, you're going to get fatigued or break down at some point. You have to be disciplined and understand and acknowledge the importance of that time off. But at the same time your mind can continue to build and build, so that once you get started again, you're away.

Going from great to great is the ultimate test in any discipline. But when you have that purpose, when you have the mental resolve to challenge yourself and push yourself to do things you've never done before, your motivation will return quickly even after you've had success. Celebrate it. Give yourself time to decompress, rekindle your motivation. Greatness beckons, though it'll be much harder than last time. Now all you have to do is be better than before.

THREE POINTS - SACRIFICE

1. Me, me, me: your purpose must be self-centred and speak to something deep within you, if you're going to be able to block out the distractions and make sacrifices in the pursuit of it.

2. Doing what's right when no one's looking is a mind game with yourself, a test of willpower. If you're serious about success, work on that willpower. Test yourself, make it a game. You'll soon see the results.

3. Going from great to great is possibly the toughest thing to do in any discipline. But don't forget that vital step in between: celebrating your success and learning to absorb what you've done before you go again.

PART III

Your Next Peak

was in Europe during May 2022 when my manager asked me, 'Are you going to go to the Classic All Blacks game?'

The Classic All Blacks are a 'legends' or 'veterans' side made up of former All Blacks, who wear the same silver fern that the Originals All Blacks side wore back in 1905. Traditionally they played a game against the Classic Wallabies out in Bermuda every year, but this time they were playing Spain's national team in front of 45,000 people at Atlético Madrid's football stadium.

Why not?

I made my way to Madrid. Tana Umaga, my old teammate and Richie's predecessor as All Black captain, was coaching the side and some of my old teammates – Conrad Smith, Luke McAlister – were in the squad. It was like coming home. It was such an amazing experience to be in that environment again. This was what I'd been missing.

I was only there for a couple of days – the other guys were there for a week – and I wished I could have been there for longer. You could see the power of the group being back together, all of us sharing stories about how life after rugby was. To be able to share these experiences with people who understood, old friends who were going through it themselves, was an incredibly powerful process. This was about more than rugby: it was a group of people who had retired, faced their own challenges and gone off into the workforce being reunited by the sport we all love. As ever, it was about something bigger than us.

We were welcomed by the Mayor of Madrid and we had a training session with Atlético Madrid, one of the best football teams in Spain. When we did a coaching clinic the day after the game, something like two thousand children turned up and we couldn't even coach because we had to sign autographs. We could hardly even get off the bus – it was like we were rock stars.

We were there to do what we could to help grow our game in a rugby-developing nation, giving back to the sport and working with the next generation. It felt like a summation of what we all faced at that moment in our lives: the keen sense of what we missed from our playing days, while also looking forward to the new legacy we had the potential to build.

That was where I found myself then: at the finishing line of my rugby career – a point at which my identity was still defined by my past – yet at the starting line of an unknown future in which I needed to leverage that past to repurpose and build something new. It's a position I know many people find themselves reaching at some point in their lives, perhaps during a period of major upheaval – whether that's as a consequence of redundancy, burnout or the failure of a business – or as part of a choice to make a change. How any of us set off from this starting line determines where this next stage of our life leads us.

*

During the process of writing this book I celebrated my fortieth birthday. It's a milestone, a moment that certainly warrants celebrating. As I discussed in Chapter 10, these occasions need to be recognised. But it also requires something else I talked about in that chapter: time to allow it to sink in. Given that I was a recently retired rugby player, at a time in life when many people in the workforce contemplate mid-career changes, I had some worries that I hope might sound familiar to anyone reading who has gone through this: *Man, I'm forty now. Am I too late to start back at the beginning again and learn over the next ten years?*

I found myself at times wishing I'd retired years earlier, so that I could have learned new skills throughout my thirties and be in a much stronger position by the time I reached forty. *This would be easier if you were thirty instead of forty . . .*

Of course, I wouldn't do anything differently if I had my time again. But the doubt, the worries, the apprehension, they're all there, making their presence felt. That voice in my head, piping up, telling me to take the easy route, not to try. After all, I've had a successful career, I could probably find an easier way to make a living than putting myself through the wringer again . . .

But if *The Art of Winning* is about anything, it's about being able to win those battles with your mind. It's about being able to strive for something where success is never guaranteed, where pressure and doubt come with the territory. It's about chasing victory when defeat is a very real risk. It's about striving to get that little bit better every day, without becoming overwhelmed by the outcome.

Nobody wants to be an 'ex' for ever. If, at some point in the future, I could be known for what I'm doing then rather than still be labelled 'Dan Carter, ex-rugby player' then I'll know I have done something right.

When I worked with Kevin Roberts on repurposing my life, throughout the process of examining who I am he was determined to get me to distil myself down to what he called my 'one-word equity'. What was the one word that would sum up my purpose in this next stage of my life?

As we worked together it became clear just how much my entire sense of identity was couched in not only being a rugby player, but in rugby terminology. It made me feel hungry to find some other ways to identify myself, to explore who I am in this next stage of my life. Through working together as long as we did, we eventually alighted upon my one-word equity: ambassador.

I'd seen myself as an ambassador for brands before, of course, but this meant something far broader, more all-encompassing – that I was, in a sense, an ambassador for New Zealand, for the All Blacks, for the game of rugby itself. The lessons I've learned through my sport that I have distilled in this book form part of this next role in my life – as an ambassador for the next generations of leaders in any field.

This concept tied in perfectly with the idea of social impact that I wanted to have in this second stage of my career: my partnership with UNICEF and the DC 10 Fund I set up, and the twenty-four-hour kickathon I did to raise money for clean water and sanitation for kids in the Pacific; becoming the first Leader in Practice for the Oxford Foundry, the university's entrepreneurship centre, where I worked to mentor the next generation of leaders on teamwork, resilience and purposeful leadership.

I'm currently not CEO material. That isn't where my near future lies. But this idea of being an ambassador and creating social impact is the basis of what Tim Brown would describe as the second peak of my career. I'm standing near the foot of it now, but the experience I've accrued throughout eighteen years in rugby gives me confidence that this peak could be higher than the first.

When you're making a transition like this in your own life, one thing I have learned is that, just as on the rugby pitch, if you have the luxury of time on your side then use it wisely. Everyone I spoke to offered me this piece of advice: 'Don't rush into anything. Take a bit of time first.' And it's true: whether you've just finished playing professional sport, you've recently been made redundant from a job you've been in for many years or you feel you've hit the ceiling in a role you should have left years ago, it can be tempting to say yes to the first thing that comes along. But if you're fortunate enough to have some time on your side, you can look at these opportunities a bit more clearly, and using the art of subtraction, truly map your next journey in line with your core values and purpose.

I said yes to too many things when I retired. Opportunities were coming my way and I thought I had to grab at them. *Who knows if they're still going to be on the table tomorrow?* And that's where the art of subtraction comes in – learning to say no to more things so that you can focus on your core purpose, the thing that gets you out of bed each day with a sense of excitement and possibility.

When you look at the next chapter of your own life, I urge you to follow the core principles of *The Art of Winning*:

1. PURPOSE

A strong and powerful personal **purpose**, to guide your way and ensure you remain swimming in the centre of your lane, even as the pressure builds and challenges mount. This purpose will be an evolution of your core values, not a revolution – just as mine evolved from the question I've spent the last couple of decades of my life asking: *What would an All Black great do?* Your purpose will describe a journey whose destination you may never reach.

2. LEGACY

Building a new **legacy**. You're part of that unbreakable chain of people going forwards and backwards in time. Once you've looked back at where you've come from, you can establish your core values to walk forward empowered by the knowledge of the past – of something far greater than only you. For me, I'm no longer an All Blacks player, but my work to enhance my legacy will continue for the rest of my life.

3. HUMILITY

To know that you're willing to be **humble,** to embrace a beginners' mindset and go back before you can go forward. When I retired, I knew that I had no right to just parachute into something at a level I wasn't ready for. I was at the starting line. You have to be humble enough to remember that.

4. MIND MANAGEMENT

Utilising **mind management.** That little voice in your head, telling you to quit, that you're not good enough, is a test of your mental strength. Find ways to focus on the present, to live in the now and quieten that voice. If you can think of it as a game, a challenge, just as I do when I'm fasting and that voice is telling me to open the fridge, then you stand a better chance of winning.

5. PRESSURE IS A PRIVILEGE

The knowledge that **pressure is a privilege.** If you aren't facing moments of pressure, forcing you out of your comfort zone, then you aren't in the business of high performance, you're cruising. These moments need to be appreciated as a product of the potential for great success. You need to learn to live for them if you want to perform at a high level.

6. RESILIENCE

A huge amount of **resilience**. There will be more setbacks ahead of you, plenty of which you can't even begin to anticipate now. But accepting that they are inevitable – that they're a part of life and that even as you stand on the verge of your greatest triumph, the rug can always be pulled from under you, you can build the mental resolve to not only weather them, but to learn from them and to come back stronger than before.

7. COMMUNICATION

Clear, precise and direct **communication**. As you ascend the ladder in any organisation, you'll soon learn that good communication is one of the key drivers of a high-performance environment. You must listen, but you must also make yourself heard. Build your lines of communication, learn to give and receive feedback and crucially *use it* to improve.

8. EVOLUTION

A constant process of **evolution**. Stand still for too long and the competition will catch you up. You must change your game, even when you're on top – *especially* when you're on top. I was a very different player at the end of my career compared to the beginning: have a growth mindset and see the evolution you can undergo in your own role.

9. IDENTITY

Know your **identity**. Only through being your real self, not ideal self, can you achieve the kind of success that is going to resonate and feel meaningful and authentic. Know who you are and celebrate that. Whether you're from a tough background or a privileged one doesn't matter, just be true to who you are. Find reasons to be grateful and listen to your gut.

10. SACRIFICE

There's no escaping this. At times I had to put my rugby career first and family and friends second to achieve the success that I did, and no one who reaches the top of any discipline does so without making some form of **sacrifice**. You can still be a good partner, parent or friend and have a top-class career, but there will be challenges along the way and difficult decisions to be made. How much you're prepared to sacrifice can be the difference between good and great.

*

As you come to the end of this book now, you are making your way to your own starting line. Whether your first peak lies before you or you're already approaching the summit of your second or third, I want you to use the blank pages at the back of this book to answer the ten questions below – to write your own legacy, as I did with my All Blacks book.

1. What are the three positive words that best describe you – and what are three positive words you would like people to say about you when describing your character?

_____

_____

_____

_____

_____

_____

_____

_____

_____

_____

_____

_____

_____

_____

_____

_____

_____

_____

_____

_____

_____

_____

2. What is something you're proud of from your past, and how can you build it into your future?

_____

_____

_____

_____

_____

_____

_____

_____

_____

_____

_____

_____

_____

_____

_____

_____

_____

_____

_____

_____

_____

3. What is the biggest mistake you have learned from and will never make again?

_____

_____

_____

_____

_____

_____

_____

_____

_____

_____

_____

_____

_____

_____

_____

_____

_____

_____

_____

4. Where do you want to be in five years? In one year?

5. What do you need to do today to start that process?

_____

_____

_____

_____

_____

_____

_____

_____

_____

_____

_____

_____

_____

_____

_____

_____

_____

_____

_____

_____

_____

_____

6. What primary state do you go into when your mind is in a state of red? Freeze, fight or flight? And what tools can you use to get your mind back into a state of blue?

_____

_____

_____

_____

_____

_____

_____

_____

_____

_____

_____

_____

_____

_____

_____

_____

_____

_____

_____

_____

7. What does your support team look like and who are they? Are you surrounding yourself with people you trust and who can challenge you to be better?

_____

_____

_____

_____

_____

_____

_____

_____

_____

_____

_____

_____

_____

_____

_____

_____

_____

_____

_____

_____

8. What is your one-word equity – the one word that sums up your purpose for this next stage of your life?

_____

_____

_____

_____

_____

_____

_____

_____

_____

_____

_____

_____

_____

_____

_____

_____

_____

_____

_____

_____

9. What are your core values?

_____

_____

_____

_____

_____

_____

_____

_____

_____

_____

_____

_____

_____

_____

_____

_____

_____

_____

_____

_____

_____

10. What are your red lines – the things you would never do?

So, what are you waiting for?

ACKNOWLEDGEMENTS

I have been fortunate in my life to be part of some great teams, and this book has been no different. I'd like to thank the following team of people who played their part in putting *The Art of Winning* together:

My publishers – Drummond Moir and the team at Ebury Edge in the UK, and Claire Murdoch and the team at Penguin Random House New Zealand.

Steve Burdett, for his help in writing this book.

Kevin Roberts, Graham Henry, Wayne Smith, Steve Hansen, Gilbert Enoka, Ceri Evans, Tim Brown, Rob Fyfe, John Brakenridge, Reid Hoffman, Owen Eastwood (Ngāi Tahu), Kaytee Boyd – for your world-class insight.

My dad, for sharing his stories about his childhood (and for allowing me to see how similar his was to my own), and to my mum, for making sure his recollections about my childhood matched hers.

Greg McGee, for the helpful feedback on earlier drafts.

Dean Hegan at Halo Sport – thanks, as ever.

I could fill another book thanking all the amazing teammates, coaches, physios, doctors and countless others who were with me throughout my playing career, and whose collective influence helped me shape *The Art of Winning*. Suffice to say, I'm grateful to all of you.

And finally to Marco, Fox, Rocco and Cruz – and of course Honor, without whom none of this would be possible.